YOU'RE THE DOG, I'M THE OWNER

Palmetto Publishing Group
Charleston, SC

You're the Dog, I'm the Owner
Copyright © 2020 by Mary Foster
All rights reserved

No portion of this book may be reproduced, stored in a retrieval system, or transmitted in any form by any means–electronic, mechanical, photocopy, recording, or other except for brief quotations in printed reviews, without prior permission of the author.

First Edition

Printed in the United States

ISBN-13: 978-1-64111-712-8
ISBN-10: 1-64111-712-5

YOU'RE THE DOG,
I'M THE OWNER

MY LIFE WITH DOGS

MARY FOSTER

DEDICATION

A gift, a blessing, a reward from God.
Thank you Trace for the sweet life I have...all because of you.
I always thank my God for you (1 Corinthians 1:4)

I truly believe our loving God brings people in and out of our lives for a reason.

Thank you Todd Bryant for coming into my life and for the support, peace and contentment you provide. You have enabled what I needed to complete this book.

PRAISE FOR *YOU'RE THE DOG, I'M THE OWNER*

Mary is a person of strength, grit, compassion, and extreme dedication. Our paths crossed many years ago when I was a young person finding my way in the world. Mary's work ethic and passion set a true example and became an inspiration for me in setting my own goals in life and also in working with dogs. She introduced me to key breeds that now fill my own home and heart. Now, as a breeder and dog enthusiast, competitor, and rescuer, I am more grateful for her guidance and friendship than ever. Mary has a huge a heart for helping not only dogs, but people, and has time and time again stretched her own time and resources to do so -and this includes myself. I consider Mary a true friend and trusted confidant. Mary has a God given talent for working with dogs and you can see her love and dedication to each one she meets. Mary looks for *and finds* the good in each dog and person that comes into her life; what an awesome blessing that is in this world.

—Kat Smith

I felt incredible anxiety leaving him for the first time. I had to go out of town for the weekend and my vet recommended Pupsi for overnight boarding. And just like that, we were off to Briscoe's (my Siberian Husky) first overnight boarding experience.

It's scary enough being a first-time dog owner. At the time, looking back on it, I had no business having a dog, yet. I was uninformed. I really had no idea how to properly raise a dog so that he could adjust to the complicated world around him. I feel bad as I look back on it. I didn't know about proper feeding, socialization, training, or even how important those things were to the health and well-being of a dog. I pride myself on being a relatively educated guy, one that researches things and makes informed decisions - and even though I thought I was well-informed before getting Briscoe, I wasn't. Like a lot of first-time dog owners, I was too focused on his cute nose, gorgeous blue eyes, and the way he playfully romped around in my lap the first time I held him.

Thankfully I met Mary Foster early on in Briscoe's life. That first day dropping him off was scary - for me, but also for Briscoe. He had just never done this before, and I had not properly socialized him to prepare him for it.

I remember Mary saying "I'd like to keep him here for a while. We can help." Tears were going down my cheek as I gathered every bit of courage I possibly could to leave my frightened little boy with a virtual stranger for an unknown period of time. But I saw a genuine love for animals in Mary's eyes. She was confident that she could help, but with equal parts compassion. I had only just met her, but I somehow knew she was going to give Briscoe the love and training he deserved.

And she did. Many times over.

She and the Pupsi team changed our lives. She worked with him daily, and equally as importantly she worked with me, in helping us adjust to our new lives together. He would have a balanced life moving forward, thanks to Mary.

Over the years, I looked for excuses to board Briscoe at Pupsi because he loved it so much. At every visit he would run toward the front door with excitement, looking forward to the love and adventures that were ahead of him.

I'm thankful for the life lessons I learned from Mary Foster, and the love and joy that Briscoe and I found because of the incredible techniques we learned from her over the years. I highly recommend her teachings for any dog lover.

—Dave Rose
Raleigh, NC

HAMPTON, VIRGINIA - 1957

"Mary, are you ready for the school bus? You really shouldn't eat Laddie's Milk Bones, they are for the dog!"

At the age of seven I was a complete dog lover. My Monday through Friday morning ritual was a constant source of pleasure and playtime with my dog Laddie. I would get ready for school, sit on the couch sharing a box of Milk Bone dog biscuits with Laddie, a collie mix. In the 1950's, Milk Bone dog biscuits were the popular dog treat, I can still remember the box. I can also remember the taste. They were almost bland with a bit of crunch. When you took a bite, it would break into a bunch of pieces in your mouth. It seemed like I was chewing on some sort of flat tasting fiber. My mother would constantly scold me, but that didn't stop me. I enjoyed each and every moment of sharing with my best friend.

I have many memories at all stages of my life with these best friends. Dogs have always been part of my life. They are incredible souls able to help mankind with many situations, problems, solutions all in day to day activities. I know my life would never have been as complete without a dog. I have always had a deep belief and faith in God and I know many of our canine friends are with us as earth angels.

Except for eating dog biscuits, I really was a perfectly normal child. From my earliest memories there was always a dog, purebreds as well as mutts in our homes and lives. I lived with my mother and grandparents in Arlington, Virginia as a young child. My mother divorced when I was just 14 months old and took my brother and me with her to live with my grandparents. I only saw my father in nearby Maryland every three weeks for a weekend visit and spent three entire weeks with him each summer.

My first dog memory was of a little Boston Bull Terrier named Kid Boots Attention Billy or Spot as we lovingly called him. My father was a great animal lover and Spot was the first dog he had bought to entertain my brother and I when we were very small. We would spend hours playing with him on our visits to my father's house.

In 1957, when I was seven years old and my brother Billy was nine, my mother decided to be more on her own and took a secretarial job at Langley Air Force Base in Hampton, Virginia. I guess my mother was in search of a more independent lifestyle. Her new found freedom gave her the opportunity to have her own place, away from any parental supervision. As an adult, I can understand her desire to be on her own, but in the beginning my brother and I sure did miss our grandparents. The gift of Laddie, our second dog, from my father certainly helped both of us with this adjustment.

Our move did not stop my loyal father from seeing us. While we no longer saw my grandparents as often, my father stayed as consistent as ever. He made the long drive from Silver Spring, Maryland to Hampton every three weeks in order to turn around and take us back with him for the short weekend. We could always count on him. He never broke a promise. I try to be the same way in my life.

My father always had a dog and I inherited his love and compassion for them. I have treated, spoiled and loved each dog I've ever had and continue to do so to this day. I also still have no problem sampling a Milk Bone just to watch the humans react.

"Kid Boots Attention Billy", better known as "Spot"

Even at a very young age, probably close to 2, I loved dogs

EARLY DAYS

I was born in Washington, DC in February of 1950. My father was a physician with an office in our home. When my parents divorced and we moved to Arlington, Virginia, our grandparents' home became ours. My grandparents were wonderful people who provided a loving, warm home. There were no pets allowed in their house, except my grandmother's cat. My grandfather had English Setters that he kept as hunting dogs but they lived outside and were never allowed in the house. When it got really cold he would fix a place for them in his garage. I especially enjoyed playing with them in the big back yard. When the leaves fell in the fall of the year my grandfather would rake them into a huge pile to be burned. I can still remember rolling around in the leaves, experiencing their texture, listening to them crunch underneath me and the smell of them when burning. All of this was shared with those English Setters. They are extremely calm and gentle dogs.

Visiting my father was a different story. Pets of all sorts were in abundance in his home. From a very early age, I remember dressing up as a nurse and treating the "sick" in my dad's office. I would sit at his big desk, climb up on the exam table, listen to everyone's chest with his stethoscope and carry his medical bag everywhere. He did more than he had to in order to attempt to be the "best Dad." He would entertain us for hours on end and our slightest whims were his desires. At his house we had rabbits, chickens with incubators in which to watch them hatch, fish, turtles, frogs and DOGS. Spot was always there to share in the activities of the day. He was a great little dog who never tired of my endless attention.

My father took us to the Washington National Zoo each spring. I was a tomboy and never bored of being with all of the creatures in the zoo. Visits with my father were always fun and something we looked forward to. He was extremely talented, very artistic and creative. He built us a lifesize playhouse. I entertained all of the animals there. Most weekend visits included a trip to the local hobby shop where I always picked out a china dog or horse for my collection.

Holidays were wonderful. My brother Bill and I always had two Thanksgivings and two Christmas celebrations. We split the day between my mother and grandparents and my father. My grandmother was a wonderful cook and would entertain the entire family: aunts, uncles and cousins. As much as we enjoyed our grandmother, we were always anxious to see our father because he always went to the extreme on decorations and toys. We had a huge train set that he had built in his basement. It was three feet high and took up half of the room. His artistic ability was displayed throughout the house. There were several different sections of the train set, with trains of all sizes and individual towns and villages, mountain ranges and tunnels for them to pass through. The detail was incredible, with street lights, ice skaters on ponds of glass, homes with windows aglow. I can still remember my father bent over his workbench. He would solder and paint all of the individual pieces that he would then display on the train board.

The Christmas tree at his home was always a delight. He always purchased the tallest tree on the lot and took hours to decorate it. There was always a mirrored "lake" under the tree with another train traveling around its base. My father had a blue neon star that he displayed in a certain window each holiday. He was a faith-filled man and I can still hear him singing old holiday songs and hymns. I guess my good memory of those words remains with me today because of his singing.

When we moved to Hampton my mother became good friends with our neighbor, a woman named Dorothy who was also a single mother. Dorothy had three children. Jaceil, Steve and Phil became our constant companions. We spent a lot of time together as my mother and Dorothy painted the town every weekend. Jaceil, Steve and my brother Bill, were in charge, and all of us were supervised by Louise, a shared housekeeper. Phil and I were the same age and in the same grade, as were Bill and Steve. Jaceil, the oldest became my "big sister" and we decided to be blood sisters. We performed the ritual with a straight pin and I still have the scar on my hand.

Phil and I were buddies and always played together. His grandfather was a sweet old man who came to visit from Florida every few months. We seemed to always be getting into some sort of trouble, fortunately it was truly innocent child's play. One snowy day we decided to hide behind some trash cans near the bus stop and play hookie. Once the bus had pulled away we happily returned home. With our dog Laddie tagging along, we went to Phil's house because Louise was at my house cleaning. Phil's grandfather promised to hide us when Louise arrived to clean their house later that morning. Our plan was foiled when she became concerned as to Laddie's whereabouts and found us hiding under the bed while searching for the dog. Doing her duty, she contacted my mother at work. Mom came home immediately and took us to school, depositing us in the principal's office with a stern warning.

That entire year with Dorothy's family was filled with many adventures and lots of fun. Laddie always had the best attitude and followed us everywhere. He was part of each adventure and our constant companion.

When we moved back to Arlington the next year we had our own home near my wonderful grandparents and were once again close to my father. After we returned to the area Laddie died. He died of distemper that first winter and the vet explained that I could not have another dog for a while until the germ was out of our backyard, so I acquired a cat. I have nothing but fond memories of Laddie. He was such an even-tempered good sport. He was always willing to do whatever was on our agenda.

The amazing train board my father built completely!

YOU'RE THE DOG, I'M THE OWNER · 9

My dad taught us to love all animals. Our rabbits, Shadrach and Meshach from the Book of Daniel.

THE FARM

My grandparents were both hardworking Virginians. They married at an early age and owned a farm in Essex County. They raised three children, then moved to Arlington after the Depression when my grandfather had taken a job with his brother in a furniture company in Washington, DC. My grandparents continued to visit the farm on weekends and for longer periods of time in the summer. It was one of my favorite places. My mother had taken a job with a defense agency in Washington, DC and my brother and I were "latch key" kids. She arranged for my uncle and one of my aunts to keep an eye on us for the few hours after school before she got home in the evening. However, she was still a single mother so we continued to spend most of our time with our grandparents.

My grandfather had Black Angus cattle, chickens, one horse, and, of course, the English Setters on his farm. I loved to visit and was perfectly content to spend my days riding around on his tractor, combine or pickup truck with him checking on the cattle, especially the newborns, going to the barn, putting out salt licks for the cows, gathering eggs from the hen house or visiting the local farm supply store. The farmhouse did not have any running water. There was a deep well that provided all the water for bathing (in the yard), drinking and cooking. My grandmother was a tremendous cook and fastidious housekeeper. Fortunately, I got her genes regarding those good habits. She allowed me the freedom to enjoy my days at the farm as long as I did my chores first.

There was a long dirt road that had a large tree about halfway from the entrance to the house. That tree was my boundary. I could walk down the road to that point and spend my time under the tree, but go no further. I have so many memories of that farm and especially my tree. Everything was so peaceful and safe there. It was nothing but happy times.

My grandfather enjoyed quail, dove and rabbit hunting. His dogs were all extremely friendly and I loved playing with them. Tony, a deep chested beautiful male and Joe, the last English Setter my grandfather had, are both part of my memories. My grandfather took his dogs back and forth from his home in Arlington to the farm. Their mode of transportation from that house to the farm was a story I have told to many people and one I will never forget. My grandfather was a sweet and caring man. He would do anything he could for you. He would pack his car for the 90 mile trip to the farm and when everything was in order and everyone was ready to go he would call his dogs by name and open his trunk. They would happily jump in and that is where they would ride to the farm. Upon arrival, the first thing my grandfather would do is turn off the engine and pop the trunk. Once again, they would happily jump out. None the worse for the wear!

My grandmother would prepare delicious meals, baking her own bread and serving homemade desserts. While at the farm she would often prepare meals from the wild game my grandfather would provide. He was not really a big time hunter, but simply enjoyed getting out with his dogs. Often, he would come back empty-handed yet satisfied from being out in the nice weather with his four legged companions. He worked hard all of his life and it seems that very simple pleasures like getting out with his dogs were the things he enjoyed the most.

Tony was killed crossing a highway after some quail and Joe died of heartworms, a disease no one had ever heard of at that time. My grandfather did not have any more dogs after Joe.

These early days of my childhood were filled with such warmth and love. I often think about those times and the lessons I learned. Not only was I raised to be kind to animals and mannerly to people, but the Bible and church were strong points in both of my families. My grandparents quoted bible verses and believed in the Golden Rule and my father read the Bible seven times in his lifetime and told us many stories from it. In both families each and every meal began with prayer. I do not think I realized how blessed I was until I got older. Saying your bedtime and mealtime prayers and listening to bible verses were a natural part of life. In my adult life I try to always remember my faith and turn to my prayers daily, knowing I will be watched over. Look what God does for the sparrow. We are more important to Him than a sparrow.

My grandparents instilled so much good in me. There are not too many days that pass by that I don't think of one or both of them. I have my grandmother's eyes and many of her excellent habits. I possess the same kind of love in my heart that made my grandfather such a noble person. They were two of the greatest blessings in my life. It would be wonderful if more people were like them in these modern times. They were such believers in family, honesty and hard work. I don't have too many relatives left, but am so proud to be related to the ones that were part of my grandparents lineage.

The farm

My wonderful grandfather and Joe, his last English Setter

A NEW FAMILY

My mother remarried in 1960 and we moved to McLean, Virginia. With three new step-brothers and my cat, Taffy, there were no dogs allowed in the house. My step-father was very devoted to my mother and did more than his share of caring for a big family. Our threesome had turned to a family of seven overnight. "GW", as I fondly called my step-father, prepared dinner for all of us most evenings. He would cook in his office clothes, not taking the time to change before pulling out the pots and pans, chopping onions, boiling spaghetti, dicing peppers. He was in a good mood most evenings, turning on the stereo the moment he walked into the house. We had a piano and he would often sit down and play a few notes and sing. He loved to dance and there was always music. The TV was in another room and did not interrupt his cooking atmosphere. Our friends always thought it was amusing to see him stirring a pot of chili in the suit and tie he wore to work.

When I was 10, and my brother Bill who was 12, decided to go to Maryland and live with our father. Bill did not take to our new family: there were now four other males in the household.

I continued to spend three weeks with my father in the summer. He always took us to Ocean City, Maryland where we rented the same room every year at a place called Fountain Court. The proprietors knew us well, and I looked forward to the trip each summer.

My father was the person who taught me all about the water. I loved the ocean and loved to swim. Our days at Ocean City always included trips to the beach. My father was athletically built and spent as much time riding the waves as my brother and I did. Our nightly activity was always a trip to the Boardwalk. Our favorite stop was a place called Nathan's. My father must have spent a large part of his salary each evening as we would spend hours pitching rings at Nathan's over clothespins. Whether I won or not, my father would continue to toss the rings until we had enough points for any of the large stuffed animals on display. I always chose a stuffed dog as a prize.

My stuffed dog collection grew and grew. Each and every one of them was special to me. Every summer was a repeat of the one before and I had stuffed dogs at my father's home in Maryland and at my home in Virginia. As for the real thing, my junior high and high school years living with my mother and step-father remained dogless.

I went away to college in 1967 and that same year my dear old cat Taffy passed away. He was 17. After a year and a summer at school, I returned home and started a summer job at the Pentagon. With the new found freedom money could buy, I decided not to return to school. Instead, I bought a car, got an apartment and of course, a dog!

Memorable experiences with my father

The playhouse my father built for us ...he was always the "best" dad

CANDY

In 1968 on a visit to the local animal shelter I found a young female German Shepherd I named Candy. The day I found her I took her to my grandparents and left her in their garage because I had picked her up on my lunchbreak and had to get back to the office. When I picked her up that evening to show my mother and stepfather, I didn't realize she had eaten an entire bushel of apples that had been stored in the garage. Her introduction at my mother's house was brief, because she had an explosive bowel movement in their recreation room on the brand new orange shag carpet. Apples, especially a bushel, work wonders on the digestive system.

Despite the rough beginning, she was a wonderful and extremely protective dog. It did not take her long to become very devoted to me and to settle into her daily routine. I would walk her each morning then leave for the office. She would be content to wait for my return home each day despite the fact that the only distraction during the long day was the mailman. I lived in a very old apartment complex in Alexandria, Virginia. The mail slots were in the front door. Candy would allow the mailman to push the mail through the slot in the door, then she would devour every piece of it. I never managed to break her of the habit because I was never home when the problem occurred. My solution to her eating the mail was to place a basket on the outside of the door in order to receive and pay my monthly bills.

Candy loved to go for rides in the car. In those days gas station attendants still washed your windshield and filled the car with gas. There was no "self service." We had to frequent different gas stations because Candy shared no love for any of the attendants. She barked and growled and if she could have come through the windshield to get to the attendants she would have.

Unfortunately, Candy went after a small poodle one day when we were out on our walk. She was on her leash but the poodle was not. When the poodle ran up to her barking, she grabbed him and shook him like a rag doll. I broke it up immediately and realized the poodle would need some medical attention, so I took Candy back to the apartment. I came back out to tell the poodle's owner that I would take care of any medical bill, and that his dog needed to get to a veterinarian. He appeared in the apartment complex with a rifle threatening to kill Candy. I was able to calm him down and make him realize that the dog needed to get to a vet and with my promise to pay for everything, he backed off. The poodle recovered, but I was concerned about Candy. After telling everyone at work about my problem, an army major I worked with offered a new home for her. I was doubtful as I knew how aggressive Candy could be. There were problems with the major's offer: his wife had chickens and raised Siamese cats! Sure enough, during her very first week on their farm, Candy killed a chicken. But the story had a happy ending. Instead of finding a new home for Candy, the understanding major's wife tied the dead chicken around Candy's neck for a few days and that solved the problem. Not only did Candy live out her years on that farm, the entire family loved her as I had, and she became the protector of the cats, chickens and the family.

Candy's experience with the chicken was an unpleasant one. With the dead chicken around her neck for few days, she could not relax, and she certainly couldn't come inside with the family. Not surprisingly, she quickly got tired of the smell, the burden and the entire situation. Once the chicken was removed, Candy associated the unpleasant experience with all of the chickens and left them alone. I have often suggested to owners of dogs that have a problem staying out of the trash, digging up the flowerbed, cruising on the kitchen counter, to make their experience somewhat unpleasant so they can learn to leave that problem behind. For example, if you use a scat-mat, a little invention that emits a small shock when a dog's foot lands on it, on a kitchen counter it should only take one or two times before the dog will no longer try to put its paws on the countertop. Placing small, set, wooden mouse traps in the top of a kitchen garbage can will accomplish the same thing. Once the dog begins to snoop in the trash and the mouse traps all go off, most dogs will not go back to explore the garbage.

Create an unpleasant experience around a bad habit and the dog will quickly associate it with the object, the trashcan, not you, the owner.

KATIE

Katie was one of the most intelligent dogs I have ever had the pleasure of knowing. She was a German Shepherd/Collie mix with a vocabulary of over 20 words! I got her in 1970 as an eight week-old pup and named her after a dog my stepfather had told me about that he and his first wife owned.

She was very protective of me and completely under my control. She understood everything I would say to her and her eyes seemed almost human. She would constantly look at me and wait for me to let her know what I wanted her to do. Owning Katie launched my future career as a dog trainer. Previously, I had completed a few courses with Candy at a local obedience school, but with Katie's ability, I got very involved in dog obedience.

Katie mastered course after course and excelled at each one. I was offered a position with the obedience school assisting with the classes, helping the individuals with their dogs, and answering questions. I enjoyed working with my dog and interacting with new people and their dogs every few weeks. Although I was a rookie, Katie made me look like an expert. She was so smart and seemed to love to work.

Katie had seven pups when I bred her to a handsome male Shepherd from Germany. She was a tremendous mother and we both shared our first experience of puppies together. A few days before the puppies were due I noticed her nesting, looking for a place to have them. I began preparations to make a place for her in my bedroom, her favorite place to be in the house. I had a chaise lounge in the bedroom that she loved. Her idea was to have them there. My idea was that she NOT have them on my favorite chair! After many conversations, she finally submitted to the place on the floor.

I stayed home from work the morning they were born. I had warm, terry towels from the dryer ready and assisted each birth by rubbing the pups all over after she had cleaned them, making sure their little throats were clear of any mucus. All of the puppies were very healthy.

I took them to our vet the next day to make sure there were no problems in the litter and to have him check Katie. The puppies were in a deep basket with Katie right beside them. I kindly asked everyone to keep their distance in the reception area as Katie was having no part of their curiosity. One lady was particularly insistent, and finally, after several verbal warnings from me, Katie ended her meddling into her new pups by biting her on the knee. The woman leaned too close to Katie's pups and her strong motherly instinct took over. Fortunately, it was not too serious of a bite and the receptionist told me not to worry, they had insurance to cover such problems.

I loved each and every one of the puppies but realized I certainly could not keep them all. The pick pup of the litter went to the owner of the sire. He had not charged me any stud fee for breeding with my Katie asking only for pick of the litter. With a job at the Pentagon and six beautiful puppies to sell, it was not difficult to find them good homes.

By this time my father had retired from his job with the Washington DC Health Department and moved to Vero Beach,

Florida. I took Katie and drove down to visit him and see his new home. An ocean lover from the days I spent with my dad each summer, I fell in love with the wide open beach and the climate. Katie and I drove back to Virginia where I quickly ended my job with the Department of Defense, terminated my townhouse lease, packed my belongings and moved to Vero Beach.

The issue of staying with my father until I found my own place presented no problems, as he was overjoyed to once again have a dog under his roof. In a few weeks I became a bartender and rented an apartment nearby. Katie easily fell into a new lifestyle of spending her days on the Atlantic Ocean. She loved the beach and would follow me out into the water as far as I would go. She would come home each afternoon after our swim, get rinsed off, and collapse. There were many nights when she would accompany me to work, because I worked until 2 AM. I had a Jeep which usually had the doors off and the top down. Katie would sit in the car and wait patiently for my shift to end. I had signs on the windshield and side that issued a BEWARE OF DOG warning for any curious passerby. The local police said the warning was sufficient. I knew Katie would not attack anyone. She wouldn't even bark unless someone put their hands on my car. If the need arose, however, Katie would jump out, relieve herself, and jump back in the car. I didn't worry about losing Katie: the only way anyone could ever take her would be to take the car and I seriously doubted that would ever happen.

Katie was so intelligent. She never required a leash and the "dog laws" were not as strict then as they are now. Oddly, she loved any word that began with the letter 'B". Anyone could tease her with words that sounded like that alphabet character, because she associated any word that started with a "B" with the beach: her favorite place on earth. She would also follow our boat back and forth on shore when we would water ski. Sometimes wanting to join in on the fun, she would just jump in and swim out to us.

One year, when tourist season ended in Florida, Katie and I packed the car and moved to Cedar, Michigan where I took a job for the summer season. We lived above a Polish deli in the small town and quickly made friends with the nice residents of the area. Cedar is located near the Upper Peninsula of Michigan and very close to the Great Lakes. When I wasn't working, we would go out on the lake, with Katie accompanying us on the boat. She loved to retrieve balls and would jump off the boat, get the ball, swim back to shore, shake the water off and swim back out again. The entire time she kept the ball in her mouth. She never tired of enjoying her life. She was my constant companion. I am confident she has a special place in heaven with a beach to enjoy. I am also confident that God sent her to me to protect me on all of the road trips we took together at all hours of the day and night.

RAINBOW

I married in 1977 and my son was born in April of 1980. My marriage was over before my son turned two. After my divorce I moved back into my mother and step-father's home in McLean, Virginia. Very shortly thereafter, we got a dog. Rainbow was a German Shepherd who had lost her mother at the age of three weeks. My son named her and quickly decided she was his dog. I think my son Trace, at the tender age of three, was a lot more mature than the dog. As it turned out, Rainbow had a lot of problems.

Of course, I had visited the breeder and heard the sad tale of the pups losing the mother dog. The puppies had been started on watered down kibble earlier than planned, because their mother was sick and could not take adequate care of them. The breeder seemed to have done a great job, keeping a close watch on the pups by keeping all of them in her kitchen and giving them all her attention. They were very fat and healthy. I had no idea at the time of the problems I would encounter with Rainbow over the next few months. In the end those problems would all be a big asset in the learning process for my future work with dogs and in the long run have provided invaluable lessons.

I had to go to work each day and Trace went to a sitter. While everyone in the house worked, Rainbow spent her day in my bedroom in a very adequate crate. I would walk her each morning, come home at lunch to walk her for the first few months, and then in the evening, first one in the door would let her out in the fenced backyard.

Unfortunately, being penned up alone all day, she became wilder and wilder. No one could get their hands on her because she would try to bite. When we let her out of the crate she ran with reckless abandon through the house, chewing on everything and trying to destroy anything she could get in her mouth. I tried every command I had learned at obedience school but nothing worked. A leash and collar did nothing, as she would dart right and left, trying to choke herself. The only time she was manageable was when she was asleep. You literally could not let her loose in the house and you sure could not take your eyes off of her.

Within a few months I found myself at the end of my rope. I called a dog trainer who made house calls because I couldn't get her in the car. Meeting Bob Maida of Manassas, Virginia was another leap in my path towards dog training. He walked into the house, observed her for a few minutes, and the first words out of his mouth were "She has no puppy manners."

For a moment I felt like thanking him for his time and paying what was due and showing him the door. No kidding, no manners! He was certainly on target on that point. I soon learned that he knew exactly what he was talking about. When a puppy loses its mother at a very young age, there is no one to correct what the pup does. In a litter, with an active mother, puppies are corrected all the time. As the puppies are weaned, and the mother leaves them more frequently, interaction with the littermates is very important. Rainbow missed out on all of this natural dog socialization. Losing her mother at a very early age, she was left on her own. Being hand fed and played with when the breeder and her family could find the time, was not enough. She missed all the developmental skills all dogs need.

It is so important for the puppies to spend time with their mother as well as their littermates. The mother instills the puppy manners. Interaction with other littermates prepares them to go out on their own more confident, more aware.

In addition, in every litter there are dominant and submissive pups. Rainbow was certainly the dominant one. Her biting was the first sign that she had never been corrected. If you have ever bred a female and witnessed the birth of pups and the next 7-8 weeks of their lives, it is easy to see how the pups are corrected and how they develop.

In the beginning, the mother is on her guard and very attentive. Her pups are her only concern. Most mothers will only leave the pups to relieve themselves, get a quick drink of water, and then go right back to them. She will only eat when the pups are quiet and asleep. At this time, the pups are no problem. She tends to their every need: food, warmth and cleanliness. As the pups grow and begin to move around, the mother may leave them a bit more, but continues to keep them warm, fed and clean. When they open their eyes they begin to move around even more. Some pups will find a favorite corner to curl up in while others may sleep on top of one another. They begin to play with each other using their paws and mouths. Ears and tails become something to investigate. The mother stops cleaning up after the pups as they develop and begin to eat puppy food.

Good breeders will take over at this point because keeping the puppy area clean is very important in their later housebreaking period. The mother will continue to bathe the pups by licking them. Once the pups are completely weaned it is important to begin to take them outside at regular intervals to get them on a schedule. It is extremely important to keep their inside area very clean. When they are about 2 weeks old, the puppies really begin to play with each other. Some sound very ferocious while others may be more submissive. Some would rather eat and sleep then romp, while some act as if their battery will never run down. Whenever their mother appears, they run to her. She will correct them when they misbehave by giving them a nudge or growling and holding them down. She will be even more aggressive when correcting them from nursing her. Once she feels they are ready to be weaned she is very consistent about stopping them from any further nursing. Her growl will become louder and she may even show teeth. She makes it clear that her milk is no longer available. If she notices they haven't eaten all of their food and decides to finish it herself, watch out! A puppy will only try to take from his mother's bowl one time. When she corrects him, by uttering a loud growl and placing her mouth on him, you may think she has broken the skin … all of this is her way of instilling manners in her pups. At times, you may think she is not interested in her pups at all, especially after she has corrected them. Many other times she will still lie down and cuddle with the pups, still licking and inspecting each one. Often mothers allow their pups to entertain themselves all day without her attention and still have the desire to sleep with them at night.

Bob Maida, who helped me with Rainbow, taught me so much about dogs. He gave me a number of lessons to work on with Rainbow and showed me how to correct her, using many of the techniques I had learned with Katie. Through some hard work, Rainbow grew into a beautiful young female, but despite all her success, she still had her destructive habits if left on her own too long. At the time I was a single mother with a small child and I worked three jobs. Although everyone in the household showered Rainbow with attention when we had the time, often taking her on long walks and for rides to the park, we could not give her enough exercise to calm her destructive tendencies. I knew all of the negative behaviors were due to boredom. I also knew if we were going to be successful, Rainbow had to find something to do with her excess energy.

 A very good friend of mine was crazy about her. When my stepfather had to have back surgery, he asked me to please find a good home for her, as he had a long recuperation at home and could not let her in and out. That's when Rainbow went to live with my friend, where she enjoyed three acres of land to run on and constant attention. She only destroyed a few items of furniture before the new routine and added exercise kicked in. With her new owner she became a very content canine and finally settled down. Many breeds require a great deal of exercise. I feel Rainbow's needs were excessive due to the loss of her mother at a very young age. However, owning her gave me the chance to meet Bob Maida. To this very day, I often quote what I consider invaluable information to dog owners or future dog owners, all acquired from the trainer that helped me so much in Virginia.

Rainbow!

RESCUES

My list of dogs continued to grow. I remarried, quit all three of my jobs, moved to Chantilly, Virginia and started a daycare center in my home. For three years I took care of the same 13 children, many of them from the time they were three months old to three years. Although busy with the daycare business, during this period I also rescued two dogs. Sandy was a retriever mix that came from the Arlington County pound. She was very light colored, almost white. I named her Sandy because she was the color of beach sand. She had the lovable, lab mentality and that is why the pound had decided to nurse her back to health once they found her, feeling with her sweet personality, she would have a better chance of being adopted. I knew from the time I saw her that she needed a home with me… full of dog love!

She was found in the woods with a piece of elastic around her midsection – probably a remnant of some type of skirt or pair of pants she'd been dressed in. Personnel at the pound felt she had possibly belonged to a family and little children had dressed her up. The elastic had been around her middle so long, that as she gained weight it cut into her skin. When I went to the pound, looking for a dog, they told me her story but would not release her for adoption until they were sure she could survive and had suffered no behavioral problems from her experience.

The pound pumped her stomach with yogurt and hand fed her until she got her strength back. She was also on massive amounts of antibiotics for the wound from the elastic. Sandy had endured much pain both from the infection and also from the vet having to physically dig the band of elastic out of her flesh. I visited her often. The entire healing process including evaluating her personality after going through the ordeal, took about a month.

At last it was time for her to be adopted. Because of my many visits and the attention I seemed to give to this poor dog, they quickly approved the adoption. Sandy was a welcome addition to our home and to my business. She never lost her sweet temperament. She loved the children I took care of and would let them lie down with her and stroke her silky coat. The children never tired of hearing the story of Sandy and her scar. Sandy never lost the wide scar all the way around her middle, but she did seem to lose the memory of it. She was a very sweet, playful dog who had a loving family and a good life. She lived with us for four years.

Sweet Sandy

BEAR

I must devote a large portion of this book to another rescue that entered my life at this time. Bear left many paw prints on my heart. He was possibly the most wonderful dog anyone could be blessed with. I am convinced Bear came to this earth as an angel in the form of a canine. No other word but angelic can describe him. I sincerely believe many dogs are angels in disguise that watch over us, keep us company, lift our spirits, protect us. I feel this way about a lot of humans too.

Bear was an Alaskan Malamute/Labrador mix. I got him from the Fairfax County pound one day when I "just had to go look" at the available puppies. He was a five week old stray with a cut across his nose. He was big, bigger than some of the older dogs in the pound. Once I was approved to adopt him, it took all my strength to carry him out of the shelter. I doubt he was ever very little.

When we left the pound I took him to Manassas Animal Hospital to get him checked out. That was when I first met Dr. Jim McDonald, possibly one of the best veterinarians in the country. He assured me Bear was in top condition and the scratch was probably from some woods dweller that curious Bear may have surprised. When Trace arrived from school that afternoon there sat Bear in the kitchen. Trace was amazed at his size and the fact that he was still a young puppy. Trace was five years old and Bear only five weeks! Bear possibly weighed almost as much as Trace and was very large. When Trace stretched out on the floor beside him the puppy was almost as long as he was. He was a perfect four legged companion for Trace as he was far from fragile. Just the type of dog a boy could roll all over, lay on and love to pieces!

On a puppy trip to the vet one day when Bear was eight weeks old he jumped out of the window of an open pickup truck my husband was driving and ran away. (I was at home with my daycare "kids"). The man I was married to at that point who had been driving the truck did stop and attempt to find Bear but when he failed he came back home and told me what had happened. I was devastated. I was so angry – why, I asked, was he driving down the road with the windows down with a young puppy? Trace and I went back to the area where Bear had escaped and searched and called his name to no avail. We stopped at two homes nearby and told the people we were looking for our dog and gave our phone number and a description of dear Bear. The area Bear had jumped from the truck was very desolate, wide open fields and only two homes.

The next morning we were preparing to go out and put flyers with Bear's picture on it in an attempt to find him when the phone rang. A very nice woman asked if I was the one looking for the dog. She said she thought they had my puppy.

I was so afraid that I would go to their house and it would not be my Bear I asked a good friend to go with me. When we arrived at the house, the lady showed us in and there on the hearth in front of a fire was Bear. He seemed unharmed but was exhausted and covered in briars and ticks! A little girl stood by with her brother and explained that she had found him. Not to be outdone the little boy quickly interjected, "Yeah, and I watered him!" I could not have been more thankful. I took Bear to Dr. McDonald who checked him out, stitched up a couple of wounds and picked dozens of ticks off of him.

When Christmas arrived that year the family who had found Bear was at the top of our list. God had his hand in everything that happened the day Bear ran away. This family certainly did not have a great deal of money and possessions. Their home was one of two that we visited the day we were searching for Bear. It was as if it was intended for Trace and I to go to that house and ask if they had seen our dear puppy. We felt we owed them a deep debt of gratitude and what better way to say thank you than to try to do something to put smiles on their faces. Cabbage Patch Dolls were the top little girl presents that year and most little boys love bicycles. So, we decided to visit them again but this time to give them a gift, as they had certainly given us one with the return of Bear. The smiles on those children's faces were an extra perk. Watching their mother open her Christmas cookies and the homemade treats we had brought was heartwarming. It really was a wonderful story and I feel surely it was God's way to help that family out at Christmas.

Bear filled our house with total love and devotion. He quickly acclimated to our family and never did anything wrong. He would even relieve himself in the same exact spot in the yard each day, as if he knew it would be easier for me to keep the yard clean, especially with toddlers playing outside. He allowed the children to do anything to him. He would lie in the sun in their huge sandbox and they would pass the time covering the dog with sand. He had to be hot, covered in sand, as he was mostly black with a very full coat, but he never seemed to mind. The children would poke his eyes, pull his tail, do the things that little kids have to be taught not to do but I never heard the dog issue anything close to a growl.

I decided to close my daycare business when we moved to Fauquier County in Virginia and I took a job as the school nurse at my son's elementary school. We lived in a new home that backed up to a wildlife preserve. Once again Bear proved to be the ever obedient dog. He had acres to roam but was content to stay at home, either in the front yard, on the deck or in the back fenced area. We had fenced the back area in order to keep wildlife out. Bear settled into the new routine of my not being at home during the day and seemed perfectly content. He would always welcome us at the end of the school day and look forward to his nature walk. Trace had a fort on the property which he had constructed from logs and tree branches. Bear was his constant companion in the late afternoons and on weekends. I never worried about anything with Bear on the property. I knew he would always alert me if anything was out of the ordinary.

My husband worked for American Airlines and wanted to investigate the Raleigh, North Carolina area. He took a transfer with the company in 1989. Trace and I stayed in Virginia until the end of the school year because I was employed by the school and Trace was in the middle of his fourth grade year when my husband accepted the job. At the end of the school year we packed up two Ryder large trucks with furniture and drove to our new home in Cary, North Carolina. It was June, 1989, and I drove one truck with Bear and Trace's rabbit, Bullet, while my mother took Trace in her car and my husband drove the other truck with his cat. As always, Bear took the shotgun seat and enjoyed his new adventure. He rode right next to the rabbit with never any thought of harming him. It was clear Bear understood the rabbit was another member of his family.

Cary, North Carolina was a beautiful place. I loved the roads, divided by lush green grassy areas, crepe myrtle trees and Bradford Pears. I took a job at a local country club and quickly worked my way up to

Banquet Manager. The club general manager told me I was overqualified for the advertised position but I knew if I could get my foot in the door I could advance. With my typing skill and command of the English language, I did exactly that. Life was very routine and working out extremely well. My mother came to live with us because I was a bit uncomfortable about Trace being a latch key kid like I had been. Times had changed since I was one. My mother got right into the routine and soon had her own network of friends. Bear had a fenced-in yard and adjusted beautifully. He was such a good dog. When I worked in my front yard, planting my beloved roses, Bear would lie on the front porch with absolutely no inclination to go elsewhere.

Bear lived the remainder of his life in Cary. The following chapters include other family members (canines) that Bear helped raise. He was never a problem when a new animal was introduced to the family. As he aged he might echo a grunt or a small growl, but no harm was ever intended. Whenever a new member came into our family he would give me a look like I had lost my mind, then accept whatever new animal was put before him. Bear was the kind of dog each family should be blessed with at least once. He actually helped raise every pup that appeared at the door. The only time I ever heard him really growl was when my husband yelled at me and put his hand on my shoulder. Bear made it clear that he was my dog and my protector. He was the pure definition of loyal.

Bear was my constant companion for almost 16 years. He rode in the car every time he could. He cried when I cried. He was a trooper, never refusing to do what you wanted him to. He was the perfect companion to Trace and always watched over him. Words cannot begin to express the dog that he was. I am convinced that Bear came to me from heaven to be an earthly creature, watch over me, and when it was time, return to heaven. There is no other place he could possibly be. From all that I have read about near death experiences, and my deep belief in the after life in Heaven, I expect Bear to be one of the first sweet souls I see when I reach that kingdom one day.

The BEST Bear and Trace

Bear

SOX

Shortly after moving to Cary we had a bad storm and Bullet the rabbit got out of his pen and ran away. We had set him up on our back deck and never realized the wind would be so bad that it would blow his door open. We were not accustomed to the hurricane warnings and watches that North Carolina gets. After losing Bullet, Trace asked if he could get a German Shepherd. I checked the Sunday paper and saw shepherd pups for sale.

Sox was a mix but his mother was a German Shepherd. He came from a local family and they were not sure what breed the father was. Trace was an active nine year old and once he saw Sox he knew he had found his dog. Sox was just what he wanted and throughout his life proved to be just a good, ole dog. He wasn't lazy but he didn't do anything that might exhaust his energy. Going for a walk or the jiggling of the car keys indicating a ride in the car didn't really excite him. What Sox really liked was to sleep and sunbathe. He loved Trace and was content to sleep in his bedroom. The living room couch was also one of his favorite spots. He got along great with Bear and just went along with anything. On our walks he was always the dog in the rear. Exerting himself or using excess energy was foreign to him. He preferred sunshine naps and quiet time. On visits to the vet, Sox was always the one "in shape" which always surprised us as he did absolutely nothing.

Sox passed away one morning in our kitchen. The veterinarian said that he "threw a clot" which is another term for an aneurism. The event was heartbreaking. My mother was eating breakfast when poor Trace walked in on the entire scene as poor Sox simply fell over and died. It was Trace's first experience with a dog's death and it hit him really hard. Sox was only nine years old, which was young for our experience with our own dogs. Throughout his life he was just a sweet companion and he certainly enjoyed the life he lived.

HOBIE

The NC State Fairgrounds with its weekend flea market was a new experience for my family. It was one of Trace's favorite places to visit on the weekends. Vendors sold puppies, kittens and rabbits at the market. One weekend, while visiting the fairgrounds, Trace came racing up to me out of breath telling me that a man was threatening to drown this puppy at the end of the day if he hadn't sold it. What a nice picture that paints in a child's mind. He was pleading with me to buy the puppy. With Trace leading the way, I went over to see the pup and the idiot who was selling him.

Hobie, a St. Bernard/Border Collie mix, was named after a surfboard, came home with us that afternoon. I kept him out in the front yard and took time to inspect him all over. He had some sort of skin condition and was very timid. I was unsure about placing him around Bear and Sox until a vet checked him out. He had obviously not been taken good care of.

Hobie came a long way in the next few months. He was, without a doubt, one of the cutest puppies ever. It took us about three months to be able to pet him without his flinching. The other dogs were completely tolerant of his shyness and never tried to frighten him. It was as though they knew the little guy had had a bad time.

Hobie's Border Collie/St. Bernard combination made for an interesting dog. If you have a hard time picturing such a mix think beautiful black and white coat, one normal eye, one St. Bernard droopy eye, BIG head, long ears and huge, tree trunk short legs. Hobie could not jump but he was ready and able to do anything else. He was very intelligent and always alert to traffic on the street and people coming up to the house. He recognized daily sounds, the postman and the next door neighbor, but was ever ready to sound off at a delivery truck or a new car or unknown person on the street. He always was alert to anything in the back yard or something that wasn't exactly right.

Hobie loved to go running with me. We would leave Sox at home and set out. The neighborhood was not as built up as it is now and there were lots of fields and good running areas. Hobie quickly learned to wait for me at each intersection. Because he was so obedient I could take him off leash and run at a good pace. He was always in front but would stop the minute I told him to and wait for me to tell him to go. When I would walk all three dogs, Bear was always at my side, Hobie on guard in the front and Sox lazily bringing up the rear.

Hobie lived a good life and stayed with us the entire time Trace was in the Navy. Trace was 20 years old when he joined the military. His first cruise was to the Mediterranean and he was gone for about six months. Trace was stationed in Norfolk, Virginia so it was easy to come home when they were in port. Hobie was always so happy to see him return. After September 11, 2001 Trace deployed to the Middle East. We found out Hobie had a splenetic tumor shortly after the deployment. I prayed daily and in each prayer always asked that Hobie remain with us until Trace returned safely home. Hobie was Trace's dog and he adored him. God granted that wish and

Hobie was able to be with Trace and the family and pass peacefully at home. He was another blessing in our lives. Hobie died on the first day of Fall in 2004. He was 15 years old.

Without a doubt, he was the cutest puppy ever!

The precious Hobie

THE NEXT STEP

In 1990, I was working as a Banquet Manager at McGregor Downs Country Club in Cary when my good friend, Dr. Jim McDonald, called to ask me how I liked North Carolina, how everything was going, and how was Bear? When I told him what I was doing for a living his response was "Mary, why are you doing that? Why don't you do what you love and work with dogs?"

I had thought about starting a dog training school when I first came to North Carolina but I really felt like I was in the South where people probably didn't do much training, at least not the kind of obedience training I was interested in. I felt there were probably a lot more hunting dogs than house dogs. But, what Jim said to me started me thinking. In truth, I wasn't all that excited about my current profession. I have always been the kind of person who can do well in a job and then get a little bored with it and move on.

I had definitely reached that point in my job at the country club. In truth, the only thing I never got tired of was dogs. Shortly after Jim's phone call, I read a book entitled "Do What You Love, The Money Will Follow". It motivated me to begin to advertise in the Sunday paper in the Pet Services and Supplies section. At first I offered dog training in individual's homes. The response was slow but steady. I began by going to a person's home, meeting their dog, listening to their list of problems and from there started obedience training on a weekly visiting schedule until the dog was trained. Slowly, I got more and more calls and even mounted a calendar on my wall to keep track of the dogs I was training. I was really enjoying it.

APRIL, 1993

"Open a storefront…you're the best investment in town!"

Many entrepreneurs would love to hear these words from a sharp accountant. My problem was I had no capital and later found out my accountant wasn't "sharp." He based his opinion solely on the growth I had shown in only four months.

When I decided to start the business I needed a name. I sat down with Trace and asked him to help me come up with a name; he has always been creative and clever. Within a few minutes he asked what I thought of PUPSI? I loved it and checked with my attorney the next day to make sure we could use the name. The business became "PUPSI, INC." and was incorporated in the State of North Carolina in May of 1993.

With one month's rent and enough money for a deposit for phone service, I rented 500 square feet of space in a small shopping center in the middle of downtown Cary. I had four good size crates to keep my students in, a small bathroom with a tub to wash dogs and a very small office. I was able to decorate it nicely with dog curtains at the windows and dog pillows on the chairs. It was very homey. I continued to advertise in the Sunday paper, happy that I could now put my training program to work.

It was the same program we continue to offer today. Owners sign their dogs up for a five day program and bring them to the shop each day. It is just like taking a child to school. The dogs spend the day with us and each afternoon the owner is given a one-on-one lesson with the dog. Everything PUPSI does is based on patience, persistence, tone of voice, absolutely no abuse, no treat training, no clicker training. Those that need housebreaking stay at PUPSI until we feel they are ready to go home. The program offers work with the dog and the owner, and has proven one-on-one over the years to work extremely well. Clients refer us to others and bring their dogs back for the daycare, grooming and boarding services we offer. When the family acquires another dog or their dog passes away, they bring the new dog to PUPSI.

In the first few months with the new store, the business was up and down. Sometimes I would have three dogs, sometimes just one dog to be housebroken. Sometime there were no dogs. I stayed at the shop, however, determined to make it work, opting not to miss any phone calls or visitors. That's when I decided to place an ad with a talk radio station. Suddenly, I was in the right place at the right time. The ad worked instantaneously. I would hear my ad on the radio and within minutes people would drive up to the shop to inquire about the training. There were no other businesses in town like mine, so you could say I was on my own and on my way.

PROBLEM SOLVING

"KINTA"

Enter the 185 lb. Newfoundland. Kinta belonged to a very nice Japanese couple who were students at NC State University in Raleigh. He was an awesome dog, very gentle and very big. He followed all of his obedience commands easily but was very stubborn about going into his "room" when our daily lessons ended. He was too large for a normal crate and at that time in my business I could not afford one large enough to accommodate him. So, I had to use my bathroom as Kinta's resting area when his lessons were completed. The room was more than sufficient, it was air conditioned, and had a half door so he could look out if he wanted to and not feel secluded from the "pack."

At that time, I worked on a short schedule with each student. Typically, the dog and I would go outside and practice certain obedience commands in the parking lot or the grassy area adjacent to the shop. Of course, those dogs needing housebreaking would be taken out on a strict schedule in an attempt to motivate them to relieve themselves at a certain time each day. After each obedience lesson, the dog would go back inside the shop where he could participate in dog daycare if he was social, enjoying the company of other canines. This part of the program was essential for their social skills. After a short time of play, it would be time for the dog to go into his kennel and I would continue on to the next student. The schedule would rotate throughout the day depending on how many dogs I had, making sure each dog got plenty of time to work on obedience skills.

Each day Kinta had a better time with the routine. His owners would arrive to pick him up, go through their lessons with him and each day he seemed to be making positive strides. He was doing great for them. However, he had a plan for me. During the day when Kinta was with me he performed all of his obedience work, but when it came time for me to work with another dog, or if I dared to do so before his daily walk around the town, where, I might add he "pranced" for the public, he would walk inside the shop and collapse on the floor. Walking all of the dogs around town each day was part of their training program to see if they behaved in public, were frightened of any street or traffic noises, and to help give them a bit more exercise.

Kinta would appear dead to the untrained eye. If I looked at him or spoke his name he would quickly close his eyes. In order to get him to move I had to put his lead around his huge neck and literally drag him into his room. Nothing could get him to get up and walk in.

Kinta excelled at his obedience and his owners were very happy. I talked with them about his habit of collapsing in order to get his way and warned them that no matter what, they had to make him do what they wanted in any situation. Kinta had figured out that his size mattered. Collapsing on the floor was his way of winning one small part of this obedience stuff.

LESSON: NEVER LET YOUR DOG GET AWAY WITH "HIS" WAY. IF YOU HAVE GIVEN HIM A COMMAND OR WANT HIM TO DO SOMETHING, YOU MUST STICK WITH IT UNTIL THE DOG GIVES IN. IF THE DOG WINS HE WILL NOT FORGET IT AND WILL CONTINUE TO BUILD ON IT. YOU BECOME THE DOG – HE BECOMES THE OWNER.

This lesson applies to dogs of all ages. Many dominant puppies will test you. Your chances of having these types of problems with a submissive dog are slim, unless you spoil it so badly that it figures out a way to pull one over on you. Dominant, submissive, puppy or adult – do not let your dog win!

FRANKIE FROM FRANKLINTON

That first summer of PUPSI was filled with really big dogs. In addition, during July it was extremely HOT. One day I received a call from a gentleman in a distant town who really needed some work done with his Neapolitan Mastiff, Frankie. The man was willing to drive back and forth each day for five straight days to have his big boy trained. I had no place to "overnight" this puppy Frankie, because he was far too big to leave in the shop, even in my bath area, and fortunately, his owner wanted him back at home each evening.

Frankie arrived on Monday morning right on time. I had just seen the movie, "Turner and Hooch" and although he was not a Bordeaux, like the dog in the movie, a Neapolitan Mastiff can strow plenty of saliva! Frankie and I would go outside and work on his obedience, then return inside to the air conditioning, ceiling fans and floor fans. Once he got in front of the fans, however, watch out! He would shake his massive head and huge strands of saliva would be slung everywhere.

Frankie however, was a great dog, extremely obedient and pretty quick, even though as a big dog it took a moment to get the command from his brain to his butt. "SIT" took a thought pattern. You had to give him a minute to process the command. Things worked out well that week, despite all the drool. I decided, however, after one too many clean ups after Frankie left that I would stick with the non-drooling breeds as my personal pets. That week with Frankie was both HOT and SLIMY!

LESSON: INVESTIGATE YOUR BREED OF CHOICE THOROUGHLY. SOME HAVE PROBLEMS SUCH AS SALIVATING SO PROFUSELY THAT THEIR CHEST IS ALWAYS WET AND SO IS YOUR FLOOR AND FURNITURE.

BUDDY, A FOX TERRIER FULL OF LIFE

I have told this story many times over the years to clients as well as many friends and family members.

A woman drove up one afternoon in tears. She walked into my shop with a cute, three month old Fox Terrier and I asked what I could do to help her. She was in obvious distress and said she had been to her vet and had a terrible experience. Apparently, the vet didn't like Buddy's manners and told her she needed to do the "alpha roll" with a dog like Buddy and proceeded to grab the little puppy and demonstrate it.

The "alpha roll" is a term many trainers, owners, and veterinarians have adopted over the years. I personally think, however, that the alpha roll should only be done on a puppy by its mother. The technique involves placing the dog on its back and holding it down in that position. Humans have adopted it to demonstrate their superiority over their dogs. When it is used by a human on a dog, I consider it nothing but bad advice. Trainers often tell owners it establishes dominance.

I don't know what I would like or not like at three months old if I were a dog, but I do know dogs do not forget anything negative from the time they open their eyes. In Buddy's case, this particular vet really demonstrated what the "alpha roll" meant. He grabbed Buddy and body slammed him down on the metal examining table and held the terrified pup down. I guess he got the submission he was seeking but poor Buddy would never forget that vet or that location.

When I got his owner settled down I told her there was hope. First of all, I advised against ever going into that veterinarian's office again as Buddy would surely remember the negative experience and probably start to quiver the minute she drove up or even worse, pee. I agreed to work with Buddy and told her we basically needed to start over to make sure Buddy trusted me, and that nothing negative, voice or otherwise, would be demonstrated.

I do not believe in negative anything. When you take your dog to a vet to be probed and felt all over it should be as positive of an experience as possible. The last thing any dog should experience is being thrown down on its back on a table or anywhere. Vets are not trainers and trainers are not vets!

I was able to calm Buddy and his owner down and she agreed to bring him back to me the next week and begin his daily training. Buddy turned out to be the sweetheart I felt he was all along. Fox Terriers are a challenge to train but most have appealing personalities. Buddy demonstrated a great deal of intelligence and an eagerness to learn. He loved his five day experience at PUPSI and I went to visit him several times in the following months at his home. His owner had labeled me a "genius" which of course I am not. I simply do not believe in scare tactics. Dogs are much smarter than they are given credit for. Many can figure you out long before you realize it. Why scare anything, much less something that cannot speak, cannot tell you what it is feeling, where it has been, what has happened to it, good or bad? With dogs, you take the good with the bad. When you decide to offer your home to a dog, you should be responsible and willing to work with whatever problem arises. If you love a dog, you understand. And, better yet, your dog understands you.

Kindness goes a long way!

LESSON: CHOOSE TO STAY AWAY FROM THE '"ALPHA ROLL" AND OTHER NEGATIVE, SCARE TACTICS. YOU ARE ONLY LEAVING A BAD IMPRINT ON YOUR DOG. DOG'S NEVER FORGET ANYTHING NEGATIVE FROM THE TIME THEY OPEN THEIR EYES. YOU WANT YOUR DOG TO RESPECT AND LOVE YOU, NOT BE AFRAID OF YOU!

This is true of puppies, adult dogs, any personality. Bad memories are not forgotten.

BJ

The eternal dog lover, I found myself at the fairgrounds one Saturday and naturally in the pet area. There was a pick-up truck with the rear area open full of little Siberian Husky mix pups. The owners had the mother and father with them. The mother was a 135 pound Alaskan Malamute and the father a handsome, 85 pound Siberian Husky. The puppies were all so active and equally adorable, I didn't hesitate to pick one out that favored my dear Bear, and brought him back to PUPSI for Bear to raise. I named him "BJ" for Bear, Jr. but within a month his ears popped up, so he did not look as much like Bear, but his name remained.

BJ was the most destructive dog I have ever owned. I cannot say his destructiveness was due to boredom because I exercised him all the time. When he wasn't accompanying me on a run, he had the entire backyard to chase birds, rabbits, squirrels and the occasional cat who made a mistake of scooting under our fence. My mother lived with us at the time and she loved BJ. She constantly fed him from the table and the scars from his massive paws in the wood of the table still remain from when he pawed the table begging for scraps while she sat eating her lunch.

Couch cushions were also one of his favorite play toys. He would wait until Mom went upstairs and then attack the couch. She never caught him in the act nor did she ever scold him. He did not learn anything from my mother except that he could enjoy different lunch entrees each day and do as he pleased in the house. He definitely dominated her. I was busy trying to get PUPSI going but would get calls from my mother to come home and find BJ. It seems he would watch for her to go out to the mailbox and scoot by her through the door and take off up the street with one objective in mind: chasing the neighborhood cats. He was not a favorite on the street.

One evening, he escaped right before I got home and when I did find him I had to get him home quickly and bathe him in tomato juice. He had treed a cat and the frightened thing reciprocated by spraying him. I was not sure if I would ever get the smell out but the tomato juice did the trick. BJ was the eternal juvenile.

In his lifetime he stood up to any size or breed of dog, killed and ate rabbits, squirrels, a snake, birds and one possum. (Thank goodness he had enough sense not to eat the possum.) We referred to him as the original NO FEAR dog. He did not show a great deal of protectiveness towards the family but predators of any sort were no match for him. He continued to destroy stuffed animals into his old age but did mature enough eventually to quit destroying couch cushions.

BJ lived almost sixteen years. In his last years he stayed under the front desk at PUPSI and would still utter a few growls if he heard a strange dog on the other side of the counter. He suffered with a bad back and eventually could not walk without falling. The day before he passed away I took him outside in the cool air and laid a blanket down on the concrete for him. He always loved the outdoors and he could enjoy smells, sights and sounds. The sun was shining and he seemed to relax a bit. It was as if God gave him a beautiful day to enjoy one more time.

> *LESSON: YOU CAN NEVER KNOW EXACTLY WHAT KIND OF PERSONALITY YOU MAY BE BLESSED WITH IN YOUR DOG. YOU NEED TO WORK WITH DESTRUCTIVENESS AND MAKE SURE THE DOG GETS ENOUGH EXERCISE TO AVOID BOREDOM. OFTEN, SOME DOGS STILL LOVE ADVENTURE AND FIND A WAY TO SHAKE THINGS UP QUITE A BIT. THESE TYPES REQUIRE AS MUCH EXERCISE AND WORK THAT YOU HAVE TIME TO GIVE. IT IS ALSO IMPORTANT THAT EVERYONE INVOLVED TRY TO DISCIPLINE THE DOG – AVOID LETTING YOUR PUP FIND SOMEONE HE CAN MANIPULATE.*

ENTER BOO

PUPSI was doing pretty well that first summer. Through PUPSI I had made a few acquaintances in the canine world, including the German Shepherd Rescue. I received a call one day from the Rescue asking for my help. It seems the owner of the Rescue had made one of her regular trips to the dog pound looking for German Shepherds and had come home with a female shepherd who had walked into her townhouse and promptly ran up the stairs only to turn at the top of the steps and "dare" anyone to try to come up there. Ears lowered, gums curled back, teeth snarling – the whole nine yards!

The rescuer was desperate. I asked her what it was she wanted me to do. "Get her downstairs and out of the house," was her reply. I had to drop Trace in downtown Raleigh at The Raleigh Little Theatre for play practice and when I related the story to him, he made me promise to take care of the dog.

When I arrived at her house I noticed the dog at the top of the stairs and took Debby, the rescuer, into her living room. She was anxious for me to go upstairs. I told her that was not the plan. The dog heard us talking and was naturally curious. She would tiptoe halfway down the stairs, peer through the stair rails and quickly run back up if she thought we had made any move. I kept talking and moving my chair closer to the bottom stair, being careful not to make any quick moves. The dog was beginning to realize I was no threat. Eventually I was able to approach her, speaking softly and gently, and loop a large collar and leash over her head. I then got her out the front door.

Debby begged me to take the dog back to PUPSI and keep her until she could place it in a home. She did not want the dog in her house because she was afraid the dog would resume her place at the top of the stairs once I left. Debby said all of the inoculations were in order and would I please, please, puleeze take the dog! Naturally, I took one long look into her big brown eyes and agreed to take her with me. Trace was ecstatic when I arrived downtown to pick him up from rehearsal with this big, German Shepherd in the car. They bonded immediately.

Boo was the name I gave her. Debby had no idea what Boo's registered name was because Debby had gotten her from the man who turned her into the pound. Apparently, he had never called her by her given name. Boo fit her to a tee, however, because she was so very frightened by any quick movements or sudden changes. Apparently, not calling her by her name was the least of the things her old owner had done to her. She was approximately 18 months old and looked as though she had never had much protein in her life. Her ears did not stand up, she had rickets and walked on the lower joints of her back legs. The poor dog could not stand up straight. All of these problems were caused by a negligent owner who did not care enough to give her any protein. Judging by her temperament, he probably was the one responsible for her timidity. The closer I got to her the more I realized her problems were from poor care and handling, not genetics.

Boo became my shadow at PUPSI. She loved Trace and loved me. She destroyed the shop her first night alone. The second night Trace and I spent the night on the floor of the shop with her. She was easily forgiven for anything she did, it was obvious she had experienced nothing but hard times until Debby rescued her.

I started her on a high protein, high fat diet. Within three months Boo could actually walk on the pads of her feet. I realized her ears would never stand but that made her all the more lovable. Her coat became shiny and she became more and more confident. She also became accustomed to routine noises in her day and no longer jolted with fear when she was unsure of her surroundings. She lived at the shop and became very protective of it. In the afternoons we walked together through the Town of Cary each day and life seemed good for the girl.

One day a very handsome man saw us walking and turned around in his car and followed us back to the shop. Although Boo was so much better, she still suffered some symptoms of rickets, and he asked what was wrong with her. He never got out of his car, but continued to ask about her and explained to me that he was a dog trainer in another town and was in Cary meeting other like businesses and leaving his business card. His training was a bit different than mine because he worked with protection dogs. I gladly took a few of his cards and promised to send any "guard dog" business his way.

Over the next few months Boo continued to make progress. She was so much better and I was so very attached to her. Unfortunately, just as we were making strides in her socialization she tried to bite a child on one of our walks, lunging at him. A few weeks later, she attacked a woman's swinging purse as the lady passed by us. It startled the poor woman and I am so glad I was so aware of Boo's problem and had Boo on a short lead. The two incidents upset me greatly and I realized I had to make some decisions. Boo lived at PUPSI and I had no other place for her to live. I could not place her with the Rescue even though she had made such great strides because she only trusted my son and me. It had taken a lot of work to build this trust, work I felt others would not be that committed to doing. She was however, becoming a liability.

I realized I had to let her go. It took days for me to come to the decision to put her down and once I decided to go through it, I spent days crying over the loss of the dog that I had nursed back to health and been there for: the dog that had learned what trust was with me. I kept asking God WHY? Why did I have to get involved with and love a dog that I had to get rid of? Why did that happen?

Why didn't I just leave her with the Rescue? Why did it hurt so much to lose her? Why couldn't there have been some other options? What good came out of it? She only got to love me for such a short time.

God does work in mysterious ways.

Whenever you continually ask yourself WHY, give it some time. I believe that everything happens for a reason and sooner or later your question will be answered. It is very clear to me why that poor old girl came into my life. I thank God for the opportunity to have known her, to have helped her get well and to have shown her love, no matter how brief of a time period. I will certainly never forget her and know she is in a much better place. I know she is experiencing true peace, with nothing to be afraid of. I am sure I will see her again one day.

LESSON: EVERYTHING HAPPENS FOR A REASON ... EVEN DOGS! ALWAYS TREAT THEM WITH THE KINDNESS THEY SO RICHLY DESERVE. YOU MAY NOT KNOW MUCH ABOUT THEIR PAST, BUT YOU CAN MAKE THEIR PRESENT AND FUTURE TIME WONDERFUL.

JACCO, A BLESSING TO MANY

Jacco was a bright eyed, super intelligent Belgian Malinois. He had worked for several police departments and ended up with the Raleigh, NC police department for five years before he was retired. One day a police officer arrived at the door of my shop and asked if I could take care of Jacco for a while. It seems he had adopted Jacco from the Raleigh police officer that had him, but Jacco did not get along with his dog, Ricky. He asked if I would be willing to take care of Jacco until he could work something out.

When I first saw the dog I thought, "He doesn't make much of an impression." But, I agreed to give him a temporary home. Jacco moved into a kennel at PUPSI. I had recently expanded PUPSI, so I had some new chain link kennels with a lot of room. Jacco was accustomed to a kennel and acclimated just fine. Over the next few weeks, Jacco grew on me. He had an amazing personality and was "fluent" in English and Dutch. His eyes were so human, they were filled with intelligence and understanding. I really enjoyed spending time with him and decided to purchase him from his former owner.

Jacco spent a lot of time with my son and me. He got along well with all of my dogs and listened beautifully. Everyone that met him was impressed with him. Tracy, the man that Boo brought into my life, came to work at the shop as a trainer and was able to work with Jacco daily, using the Dutch commands the dog was accustomed to. Once again, the now retired K-9 was back doing bite work, retrieving his beloved "kong" and loving each day he got to spend doing his old "job".

Jacco's personality prompted me to get another Belgian Malinois. Even in his retired state Jacco fathered 10 pups. Their mother Pearl was every bit as intelligent as Jacco and their family was superior. These two dogs formed the groundwork of my love for the breed.

Jacco eventually went to live with a single mother and her two young girls in Cary. They were able to provide him with a warm, loving home life. He was able to again fill a K-9 role and watch over and protect them. He fulfilled his career both on duty and in retirement…he took care of policemen and private citizens until he passed away. I believe this dog knew humans all the way to their souls … he was never wrong about a person.

> *DOGS CAN FILL ALL KINDS OF NEEDS. DOGS CAN PERFORM ALL KINDS OF JOBS. DOGS CAN BE SUPER INTELLIGENT. HOWEVER, MANY OF THESE OUTGOING BREEDS TAKE A LOT OF WORK AND PLENTY OF PATIENCE, ESPECIALLY AS PUPS. DO YOUR BACKGROUND WORK. KNOW AS MUCH ABOUT THE BREED AS YOU CAN.*

Combine a dominant dog or pup with a super intelligent mind and you will have a task on your hands. You must teach this type of dog what it is you want and expect out of him. A more submissive temperament mixed with intelligence will be a bit easier to work with.

CONSTRUCTIVELY EVICTED!

By 1995 I had expanded from my original 500 square feet to almost 1200 in the same shopping center. At the same time, the Town of Cary was growing fast and new construction plans followed. When the area where I trained and walked my dogs was going to become a two story shopping center, I began to look for another location. Fortunately, there was a one story brick building right across the street that had a large parking lot out back. With a lot of hope in my heart I approached the landlords and explained what PUPSI did ... often a very hard sell to a landlord. We were able to work out a lease with a five year term and PUPSI moved in soon afterward. It was a very easy move because all we had to do was walk the dogs across to the new building. I remember telling owners to drop them off at the old PUPSI location but to pick them up at the new location.

The greatest part about the fourth expansion was the outside area. Indoor daycare became obsolete at the new PUPSI. We were able to fence in the parking lot, the dogs loved it. From 1995 to 2004, that old building in the center of town helped the business grow.

WINTER, FOLLOWED BY STORM

Shortly after our move, a nice couple brought me a little Maltese with a big housebreaking problem. The husband was not real crazy about the Maltese. He owned and bred Siberian Huskies. As it turned out, the Maltese was not that difficult to housebreak and I finished working with him in just a few days. The owner was thrilled and a few weeks later on a Saturday morning when I was at work, the couple appeared at PUPSI with a six week old little female Siberian Husky pup in their arms. They wanted to give her to me for helping them with their Maltese.

Winter was a beautiful example of her breed with sky blue eyes and a black and snow white coat. She was a calm little puppy and often slept on our laps at the shop or occasionally went home to spend the night with a certain employee that adored her. Huskies are typically very clean dogs and she was absolutely no problem to housebreak. She was born outside and lived outside prior to coming to PUPSI so the outside area was her preference for going to the bathroom.

I enjoyed her personality and her endless energy so much that one year later I called the Suttons to see if they had any other puppies available. Sure enough, they did. I purchased a female from them and named her Storm. She and Winter had the same parents, and were only a year apart. Storm had brown eyes but in one of her eyes there was a touch of blue, resembling a sky right before it rains.

The two dogs became fast friends and have been together since I brought Storm to PUPSI. They sleep in kennels next to each other and have remained free of any housebreaking problems. The kennels they have are the same ones they started with. They are eleven and twelve years old now and the best of friends.

At the time of this update, Winter and Storm have both passed away. Both lived to be thirteen and had wonderful lives. They passed away within one year of each other. I believe Storm missed Winter so much she just gave up. They were so very close and will never be forgotten by any of us.

KIPPER

A lady called with a 12 week old Siberian Husky male that needed obedience and housebreaking. These pups are one of the cutest breeds, making them very hard not to love. Kipper arrived all full of himself and breezed through his week of training. Siberian Huskies are very clean dogs and housebreaking is not usually much of a problem. As with most housebreaking, the owner needs a lot more training than the dog.

Kipper's owner called me in four days and asked how he was doing. I told her he was all done and would be ready to go home the next day. Her reply surprised me. She told me she would not think of asking anyone but me but, would I consider keeping him? She said her house had been so peaceful since Kipper had come to PUPSI and her cocker spaniel was so much more relaxed without the young puppy at her home that she didn't want him back. I readily agreed to take him. After all, he was one of my top favorite breeds! She paid me for his training, brought me all of his things, including his AKC papers, and Kipper was mine.

Kipper is ten years old now and remains a solid fixture at PUPSI. He is still a beautiful dog and completely part of the pack at the kennel. He, like my girls, Winter and Storm are very close to me and the PUPSI family. He enjoys his life at the kennel and I am so thankful his owner asked me to take him and he was never sent to a shelter, like so many other unwanted dogs.

DUSTY, A LITTLE SIBERIAN HUSKY THAT BROKE MY HEART

Although I enjoy most of the dogs I work with, every now and then a dog comes along that I grow really attached to.

Dusty was the cutest Siberian Husky puppy and had a personality that just reached out and grabbed you. I own three Siberians, so I am already attached to the breed. I've trained a bunch of them, but this dog was almost human. He was a three month old pup with the brightest eyes and the sweetest disposition I'd ever seen. He was all dog and ready to go!

Dusty stayed with me for one week of training and housebreaking. He excelled! When his family arrived each afternoon to pick him up, they were thrilled with his progress. Siberian Huskies can be a tough breed to train and it is extremely important to begin with them at a young age … three months is not too early. They can be so aloof that you often think you are not getting through to them at all. Dusty was different. Not only did he have the outgoing personality of the breed, but he possessed actual intelligence. He was a quick learner and seemed to enjoy what he did. It was almost as if he was showing off. He would prance around as if he was truly proud of his training accomplishments.

He finished his training in five days with no problems. The family did their homework each night and as much as I wanted to, I had no excuse to keep him longer for training. He had definitely graduated. So, he left PUPSI on Friday. I really missed him after he was gone. He was, as I later found out, a little dog "angel" straight from heaven.

The following Tuesday I received a call from his grieving owner. The family had left Dusty in his kennel on Monday when they went to their jobs and to school. The wife went home at lunch to let him outside, play with him and return to work. She put him back in his kennel with his collar on. Being the affectionate little puppy he was, her leaving was not in his plans. Apparently, once she left, he jumped and jumped, attempting to get out of the crate. His collar became hooked on one of the metal parts. Dusty hung himself.

I cried for weeks over the loss of this puppy. The family cried. It was such a tragedy. A few months later, the family got two Siberian puppies and I trained them as well. Dusty touched all of our lives for such a short while.

THERE IS A SERIOUS LESSON IN THIS STORY. DO NOT LEAVE YOUR DOG WITH HIS COLLAR ON UNATTENDED. DOGS AND PUPPIES CAN GET INTO SO MUCH. COLLARS CAN GET HOOKED ON LOTS OF THINGS. PURCHASE KENNELS THAT ARE WELL MADE. LOOK FOR ANY LOOSE FITTINGS. REMEMBER THAT YOU ARE LEAVING YOUR DOG ALONE AND CHECK EVERYTHING. PUPPY PROOF YOUR HOUSE. SAFEGUARD YOUR DOG.

This warning should continue throughout your dog's life. Remember, dogs can get into anything when left alone. Make sure their environment is safe and secure.

"WE LOOK IN PAPER, WE SEE AD, WE GO SEE PUPPY, DOG IS CUTE, WE WANT, WE BUY!

This is another story with a good lesson. The quote above is almost verbatim of what I was told over the phone one day by a couple who desperately needed dog training. They had done exactly what they said. They wanted a dog, they looked in the paper, went to look at the pups, liked them, bought one. They didn't even know what a Golden Retriever was!

When I met their "pup" I found a dog in great need of obedience. The owner's, not surprisingly, needed more! This golden was completely out of control. The owners had been taken advantage of by the breeder. They obviously did not know where to begin or what to look for in their search for a cute puppy. I worked with them daily and continued for eight days. Finally, they understood what they had purchased, the commitment they must make and the daily obedience they had to do to keep this once "cute" little puppy under control. They had to continually win in each situation to keep this dog from taking over and dragging them down the street, jumping up and standing on them, tearing at their clothes. The best part is that they were willing to do this and not send the dog to the shelter.

Unfortunately, many people end up in exactly this situation. Even if they know what kind of dog they want, they do not have the desire to "work" with the puppy. So many "cute" dogs end up at the shelter because of their owner's non-commitment.

GET GOOD ADVICE BEFORE YOU BEGIN YOUR SEARCH FOR THAT PUPPY. ASK QUESTIONS AND GET ANSWERS FROM REPUTABLE TRAINERS. DEDICATED INDIVIDUALS IN THE "DOG" BUSINESS WILL TAKE THE TIME TO ANSWER YOUR QUESTIONS AND HELP YOU FIND THE BEST BREED OR MIX, WHATEVER YOUR DESIRE. DO YOUR HOMEWORK BEFORE YOU GET YOUR DOG ... MAKE SURE YOU ARE COMMITTED TO DO WHAT IT TAKES.

If you desire a pound puppy or adult dog, ask questions. If you are unsure what breed(s) your new dog is made up of, ask your veterinarian. Research each breed.

TOO PROTECTIVE

One of the biggest mistakes owners make with their dogs is being too overprotective. I find this particularly true with the smaller breeds. However, I have seen some dog owners with larger breeds who act as if their dog is completely helpless.

Everyone should love their dog and want to be a good owner. However, some people get very confused about letting a dog be a dog. They seem to think their dog, no matter what size, is almost helpless. Actually, when you really think about it, dogs can survive without us. Thankfully, we have domesticated them and they are welcome, wonderful companions in many of our lives. Unlike a newborn or small child, a puppy can make his way in the world if he has to. I am grateful to the many organizations that have hard working employees as well as volunteers that work endless hours to rescue and treat so many animals that are without loving homes.

When someone decides to offer their home and love to a dog, they usually are full of good intentions. A problem can arise when the human feels the dog cannot be left on his own, cannot walk without assistance or must be carried everywhere, has to have human food vs. dog food, and even eat at the table. Believe me, this does happen. I had one client who treated her large breed puppy as if it were a human baby. The dog went on walks in a baby carriage! She was even considering diapers until I explained the skin on the dog needed to breathe. Owners who are extremely overprotective are usually against any type of dog boarding or socialization. Unfortunately, if the owner sticks to his guns and never boards their dog nor socializes it, they end up with a dog that may become fearful of anything other than its home or owner. When and if an emergency arises and they must board their dog, it is usually a huge problem for all concerned. Socialization is so very important.

When we have such a customer come into PUPSI it is easy to realize within a few moments that we have a barrier to break down. Usually these customers bring their dog in because they have failed at any type of training and the dog has definitely taken over their life. To attempt to convince such an owner that their dog needs socialization as well as training is just the beginning of the hurdle. The thought of their dog playing with other "dogs" strikes fear in the owner's heart. These are usually the type of owners who walk their dog down the neighborhood street, see another dog coming their way and immediately pick up their dog.

If we are successful in getting one of these pups into dog daycare, we must be prepared to go through a daily drill of what we are going to do with the dog, what if it is cold outside, what if it is raining, does the dog seem scared, does the dog get a nap. These questions go on and on, often for a few weeks, until the owner begins to calm down. Eventually, the dog will arrive each day eagerly dragging its owner through the door. If the owner doesn't give in to the demands of the dog to let him go play with his kennel friends but instead begins the grueling ritual of daily questions, then the pup usually tries to leap out of her arms into the waiting arms of a kennel attendant. At the end of the question and answer session the owner finally surrenders the dog's lunch and goes off to work. You can almost see the dog give an exuberant "YES"! as the owner leaves.

Training these dogs is easy. The hard part is training the owner. We stress the use of tone of voice in working with any dog. Many of the owners that are too protective have a very difficult time using their voice in any derogatory manner. They just cannot talk sternly to their dog. They cannot stress any disappointment in their voice. We explain how important the use of your voice is in training the dog. We never want an owner to yell at a dog, however, there are many times when the owner must be serious and project that to their dog. Dogs can tell just by your tone of voice if you are pleased or not too happy ... like when you walk in and your favorite couch pillow is destroyed or the kitchen trash is all over the floor. It is very difficult to teach the overprotective owner just how to use their voice with their dog.

Another area we work on is convincing these types of clients that their dog is going to be happy to see them when they return. No matter what, the dog is going to love its owner, especially the types that have already showered them with nothing but positive reinforcement and endless affection. Dogs love you. They bonded with you when they arrived in your home. Whether you adopted a puppy or an older dog, once that dog started living with you, the bond began. (I have this certainty that you would not have picked up this book if you were cruel to animals, so I can assume your dog is bonded with you).

IF YOU HAVE A DOG OR A PUPPY, YOU WANT IT TO BE AS WELL ROUNDED AS POSSIBLE. YOU NEED TO FAMILIARIZE YOUR DOG WITH DIFFERENT NOISES, OTHER DOGS, OTHER PEOPLE. YOU WANT YOUR DOG TO BE ABLE TO RIDE COMFORTABLY IN A CAR, TAKE A LEISURELY WALK, ACCEPT YOUR FRIENDS AND NEIGHBORS. LOVE YOUR DOG TO THE EXTREME, BUT LET YOUR DOG BE A DOG.

Dominant adult dogs as well as pups are easier to socialize and introduce to new situations. You will have to work a bit harder with a submissive dog or pup.

JOJO'S FAMILY

Jojo is a little schnauzer with a growl that will scare most kennel employees. However, his growl is more for scare tactics – much worse than his bite! Jojo started coming to PUPSI after his owner decided she wanted to make a change in kennels. He became quite a regular.

One day when he was being dropped off for boarding, his owner started crying and asked me to pray for him and his wife Kay. I learned that Kay was very sick and her husband was obviously very devastated and confused about all of it. I felt complimented to be asked to pray for them.

God works in such mysterious ways. I found myself thinking of them on a daily basis. I pondered over all the things that happen in our lives that should make us so very aware of our Lord and Savior. I felt like such a small being, knowing everything that happens in our lives, is up to God. His will, not ours. His yes, His no, His maybe. However, I continued to keep them in my prayers.

People come in and out of PUPSI everyday. This was not the first sad story we experienced. In our busy schedule, we all need to remind ourselves to slow down and recognize the needs in others. Often one kind word to another is all it takes. You never know what kind of imprint you might be making. How unfortunate it would have been if I had been in a bad mood or too busy to take the time to talk to Mike about his wife.

Kay passed away a few short weeks later. PUPSI was created for dog's problems but it makes me feel special that in a small way we help with "people" problems too.

THERE IS A LESSON HERE – TAKE THE TIME TO BRIGHTEN SOMEONE'S DAY AS OFTEN AS YOU CAN. LISTEN, OFTEN YOU MAY BE THE ONLY ONE WHO GIVES THEM ANY ATTENTION.

BRISCOE ROSE

Briscoe is an energetic, fun loving solid white Siberian Husky. When he first visited PUPSI at the tender age of three months his personality was not what it is today. He arrived for dog daycare but quickly became a student. When Tracy reached in to get this cute little white ball of fluff, he lunged at and took a good chunk out of Tracy's hand. I quickly assisted Tracy and we got the scared little growler out of the kennel. At this point, Briscoe became "our project."

Dave, Briscoe's owner, is a very laid-back, quiet and calm individual. We explained that Briscoe needed socialization IMMEDIATELY. Our answer to all of Dave's questions was to leave Briscoe with us for training and to return in about five days. Dave agreed and little Briscoe's training with a strong emphasis on socialization began that moment.

It didn't take long to get Briscoe into the PUPSI routine. Our two husky's, Storm and Winter, recognized the little guy as one of their breed and naturally helped with the process. I have seen the same thing happen over and over again. Dogs seem to recognize breeds. My two huskies will always notice and warm up to another husky on the playground. It happens very often between like breeds that have never seen each other until they are playing together. Briscoe loved the interaction with Storm and Winter and they seemed to realize that he was young and needed help. They helped him get over his lack of trust with other dogs and Briscoe began to play as a puppy should. He was picked up and handled by the PUPSI staff and quickly learned that each day was a good day. He forgot all about being scared and not trusting. His training went beautifully and just reinforced the meaning of trust to him. By our constant handling and praising him when he learned each command everything was positive in his little life. With us he had no bad experiences, and there was nothing negative in his world. He learned quickly and became a natural at playing with other canines. To this day, Briscoe is a regular client and has never shown any of his original aggression. He truly enjoys PUPSI, running in the door every day and wagging his tail. He associates PUPSI with all things pleasant and actually sings for his supper when he is boarding there. His owner Dave has worked with him, involving him in many situations, all in an attempt to keep him social and to extend the training he's had at PUPSI.

Briscoe was helped at the crucial time in his development. If Dave had done nothing, it would have taken quite a while to turn him around. Fortunately, Dave made the right decision for him and his new puppy.

MANY THINGS CAN MAKE A DOG OR PUPPY SCARED. DOGS DO NOT FORGET ANYTHING NEGATIVE THAT HAS HAPPENED TO THEM FROM THE TIME THEY OPEN THEIR EYES (AROUND 3 WEEKS OF AGE). ACTING QUICKLY ON

NEGATIVE BEHAVIOR IS THE ONLY WAY TO BE SUCCESSFUL WITH IT. WHEN A DOG IS THREE MONTHS OLD THE LIKELIHOOD OF CHANGING THE NEGATIVE BEHAVIOR IS HIGH. THE LONGER YOU WAIT, ALLOWING A DOG'S BAD HABITS TO BUILD, THE BIGGER PROBLEM YOU WILL HAVE.

ONE OF THE BEST THINGS YOU CAN DO IS BE AWARE OF ANY BEHAVIORAL PROBLEMS AND ACT ON THEM. IT IS NEVER "CUTE" FOR A PUPPY TO GROWL, BITE OR SNAP. DON'T EVER ENCOURAGE THIS TYPE OF BEHAVIOR. ALTHOUGH PLAYING TUG-O-WAR WITH A PUPPY IS FUN, IT DOES LEAD TO NEGATIVE BEHAVIOR. INSTEAD, THROW A FRISBEE OR A BALL. ENCOURAGE YOUR DOG TO ENJOY GAMES WHERE HE BRINGS YOU THE OBJECT TO BE PLAYED WITH AND YOU THROW IT FOR HIM.

NEVER LIE ON THE FLOOR AND LET YOUR DOG WRESTLE WITH YOU. IT ENCOURAGES BITING AND GROWLING. IT MIRRORS THE SAME SETTING AS A GROUP OF LITTERMATES WHO TUMBLE TOGETHER, FIGHT AND BITE. THE MOTHER DOG IS THE ONE WHO DISCIPLINES THEM. UNFORTUNATELY, IF YOU KEEP UP THE SAME TYPE OF BEHAVIOR WITH YOUR PUPPY IT IS IMPOSSIBLE FOR HIM TO UNDERSTAND THAT IT IS NOT THE CORRECT THING TO DO ... SO DON'T DO IT!

A dominant pup or adult will be harder to correct than a submissive one in this area. It is especially important not to reinforce any of this type of behavior in an adult dog. Adult dogs who growl, bite or snap may be better worked with a trainer involved as they have apparently had this problem for a while. Stopping a puppy from these types of negative behaviors is quicker and easier the earlier you begin the training.

SPANKY – THE MINI CHIHUAHUA THAT ROARED

Spanky came to PUPSI for training and housebreaking. He was all of two whole pounds and despite his small size, absolutely ruled his household. He had been taken from his mother and littermates at the too young age of four weeks and given to his owners by a breeder. When I heard the story I was not too surprised as some so-called "breeders" can do some unbelievable things. Being so tiny, his new owners had to bottle feed him and little Spanky never learned any puppy manners or instruction that would have been instilled in him by his mother.

Spanky became the owner in the home very quickly and by the time he arrived at PUPSI at the tender age of five months, he was able to bite his owners whenever he felt like it, disliked all strangers and absolutely refused to wear a collar or to be placed on a leash. The one "good" trait he possessed was enjoying the company of other dogs.

As tiny as he was, no one could use any "corrective jerk" training. His neck would have snapped like a wishbone. By the second day at PUPSI, I purchased the smallest harness I could find as well as a light weight leash. Outfitted with "skitzy" gloves that we had previously used with Shar Pei's and Chow Chows, we began the task of getting the harness on Spanky. Skitzy gloves are used by dog trainers and handlers that typically are exposed to dogs that may bite. They are thick gloves that reach up to your elbows. If a dog bears down on your hand it is easy to get your hand out of the glove quickly if it seems the dog might break through the hard leather. They are extremely well made but some dogs could, with time and effort bite through them. For the most part, they will protect your hands. In Spanky's case, he barred his little teeth and growled but there was no danger of anyone getting bit. We were, however, not going to give in to any of his demands. He had had five months of people giving in to his every whim. In about 15 minutes protected by the gloves we had the harness on him as well as the leash.

His training began. I took him outside in the sunshine and grass and in about five minutes he was ready to run and play. He warmed right up to the training session and set about to show me just how smart he was. In no time at all he was heeling and sitting. No treats involved. I simply trained him the way I train all other dogs, and he learned so quickly.

As each day passed he made great progress. Housebreaking was not much of a challenge and allowing everyone at PUPSI to handle him was a smooth process. If he even let his old personality surface by pinning his ears against his head and staring at you he was quickly corrected with a firm "no" and a jerk on his harness. There was no danger of harming him with this type of correction.

When his owners arrived to pick him up on Day Five I had a long talk with them. His female owner asked a lot of questions. She had been the one Spanky had totally dominated by biting and breaking her skin. I warned them not to be at all surprised if Spanky came home and started all of his negative behaviors again immediately.

They could not give into him and under no circumstances were they to remove the harness and leash. It is very common for a dog to get back on its home turf and think it can easily slide back into former negative behavior. After all, the dog always got away with bad behavior at home in the past. Dogs are smart, the do have memories. Owners must be ready to intercede and not allow the past behavior to surface or be accepted at any time.

We went outside with the owners and had a very successful training session. Spanky excelled and showed his owners just how smart he was. He was a perfect gentleman.

The next morning I had a call waiting on my phone's message system. Spanky had gone ballistic on them soon after arriving home. He had bitten his owner's finger so hard she could barely remove it from his mouth. When I called I fully expected I would have to get in my car and go over to their house. Thankfully, he was better by the time I called and the owner's were making progress. He had reverted to his old routine but with the owner's not giving in, soon would discover he had no other choice but to be the dog, not the owner in the household.

MEN AND WOMEN TEND TO REALLY SPOIL THEIR DOGS. THAT IS FINE BUT THEY CANNOT GET THE ROLES MIXED UP. ANY SMART DOG WILL IMMEDIATELY TAKE OVER GIVEN THE CHANCE. I'VE HEARD SUCH COMMENTS AS "I'M AFRAID TO TALK LOUDLY, I'LL HURT HIS FEELINGS" TO "I JUST CAN'T JERK ON THAT LEASH". I TRY TO EXPLAIN THAT USING A DEEPER, SERIOUS VOICE WILL NOT HURT THE DOG. JERKING THE LEASH TO GET THE DOG'S ATTENTION

DOES NOT HURT THE DOG. WHEN ONE DEVOTES THE TIME TO WORKING WITH AND TRAINING THEIR DOG, WHAT IS THE RESULT? RESPECT. DOGS LOVE TO LEARN AND LOVE TO BE PRAISED. A DOG CAN TELL IMMEDIATELY IF YOU ARE HAPPY WITH THEM OR UPSET. DOGS LOVE TO PLEASE. THEY ADMIRE YOU. TEACHING THEM RESPECT IS A GREAT GIFT. YOUR DOG WILL LOVE YOU FOR IT.

Once again, spoiling a dominant, intelligent adult or pup will only reinforce his ability to be the "top dog" in the family. While submissive pups and dogs are a bit easier to spoil, as they tend to look at you with those puppy dog eyes as they snuggle up against you, be careful. If they get one up on you, they will learn to try it again and again. Love them all, but teach them with that love.

SADIE, OREO AND A BUNCH MORE!

Quite often clients come to us with the complaint that their dogs seem to be at ease and enjoy other dogs but when they are on a leash, most times for a walk, turn into a possessive growler, showing quite the opposite personality. Nine times out of ten the problem is the owner, not the dog and most often this behavior happens when the owner is a female.

Sadie was a little golden mix of something and Oreo was a black and white extremely cute mix. Both were absolutely wonderful on the playground but came to PUPSI because they turned into nightmares on Elm Street. Their owners were becoming terrified of walking them because they were afraid other dogs might attack or their dog might attack. Through lots of explaining and convincing the owners to calm down, walking both became a success. In these cases, the trainer needs to ask a lot of questions. Most of the answers are yes. Are you immediately nervous when you put the leash on your dog to go for a walk? Do you begin to look for other dogs as you are walking? When you spot another dog do you feel yourself becoming jittery and want to turn and run home? Once these owners get control of these types of situations walks will continue to go smoothly and as time passes they will forget all about them ever occurring.

If the dogs show this type of behavior while on a leash it may be because the owner is nervous. Nervous humans put out a scent that dogs can smell. When this happens, the dog thinks he must be on the alert for whatever is bothering his owner. Combine this alertness with a walk, and the dog naturally feels any other dog they meet must be a threat.

We teach these owners that they must relax, telling them they need to be one step ahead of their dog. When going for a walk they need to enjoy it, talk to their dog, use an uplifting voice. If they see another dog on a walk, they need to move to the side and pet their dog or continue to walk by, discouraging any negative behavior. The most important thing is to be relaxed and not feel there is any type of problem. Often it takes a few days of accompanying them on a walk, but we know it works. We explain that the owner needs to be in control, think of pleasant things, simply enjoy this time spent with their dog.

When these doubting owners bring their dog to PUPSI and we are able to show them their dog playing with other dogs, it helps reinforce the nervous owner syndrome and hopefully makes the owner realize that their anxiety is causing the problem.

MOST RESPONSIBLE DOG OWNERS WILL LET YOU KNOW IF THEIR DOG IS UNFRIENDLY WITH OTHER DOGS. MOST RESPONSIBLE DOG OWNERS WILL MOVE THEIR DOG OUT OF YOUR WAY SO YOU CAN PASS IF THEIR DOG DOES NOT LIKE OTHER DOGS. BY NOT

> *BEING NERVOUS AND BEING CONSISTENT WITH YOUR DOG WALKS, OVER TIME THE WALK WILL BE A GOOD PART OF YOUR DAY AS WELL AS YOUR DOGS ... A PLEASANT EXPERIENCE. RELAX! OVER TIME YOU WILL NEVER EVEN REMEMBER YOU HAD A PROBLEM.*

This is important to all dogs, puppies, adults, dominant or submissive. Consistent, pleasant experiences equal positive results.

PAYTON, A REAL CHARMER AND A DEFINITE OWNER!

Most dog lovers have seen the movie Benji. At the tender age of four months a dog named Payton arrived at PUPSI for training. He had the attitude of an old timer with a very strong resemblance to Benji and the intelligence of Tramp in the popular Disney classic, "Lady and the Tramp." Of all the dogs I have trained Payton was definitely a top dog, owner of the entire household.

Payton was a mixed breed, part Wheaten Terrier and part something else. Even his vet had not decided what he was. However, Payton had no problem naming his identity…the BOSS!

His owners had rescued him as a mere babe, and I am sure he was adorable. I know he was cute when he came through the doors at PUPSI.

One trainer took him out for a training session and came back in to inform me he was horrible. I took him out and decided he was workable, not that bad. He constantly tried to cross over in front of me, nip at my shoes, jump, lag behind, completely ignore me, you name it. I had worked with Wheaten Terriers in the past and knew how difficult they could be. I, however, was ready to face the challenge.

He did pretty good the first day. And on the whole, Payton actually did very well during the training week. On the other hand, he tried his best not to do anything for his owners when they arrived each day. Over time he gradually understood he was not going home in the evening until he did as he had done for me all day long. He was an angel at PUPSI but when his owners arrived he slipped into another costume. He almost enjoyed making them work for his performance.

Of course I talked and explained and explained why they must be serious about their commitment to training and why jerking his neck was not harmful and why they could not let him get away with anything. Each evening was a task for them and I know they wanted to throw in the towel. Payton was actually coming around for them and understanding his place.

Payton was a dog that had the intelligence to immediately figure out things and take right over before his owners knew what was happening. He would have continued to run the house and get away with all of his negative behavior if they hadn't brought him to us. His owners had no choice but to make a huge change and stop pampering him. Payton would have become obnoxious to be around if his owners had not become the boss.

WITH TIME AND CONSISTENCY, ALWAYS MAKING THE DOG DO WHAT YOU HAVE ASKED, YOU WILL WIN. AS WITH PAYTON IT CAN BE A TREMENDOUS BATTLE OF WILLS. DO NOT GIVE IN. WITH AN OWNER ALWAYS WINNING, YOUR DOG HAS NO CHANCE TO BUILD ON NEGATIVE BEHAVIOR AND BECOMING A GOOD DOG WILL BE THE RESULT.

MANY DOGS TAKE A GREAT DEAL OF WORK, TAKE A LONG TIME TO MATURE AND CONTINUALLY TEST YOU. A DOG IS A LIFETIME COMMITMENT, NOT A FIVE DAY ONE! YOU SHOULD NOT OWN A DOG IF YOU ARE NOT COMMITTED.

Payton was a perfect example of a dominant, intelligent pup. If his owners had not committed a great deal of time in continually working with and correcting him, they would have had a real problem on their hands.

RALEIGH

Raleigh was another one, determined to be the boss, one way or another. He was a little mutt found on the streets of Raleigh, NC and appropriately named. He was an "attitude plus" little dog and seemed to truly enjoy his role as a canine. Of course he needed obedience training and was no small challenge. While showing his owners that "unconditional love" thing, letting his good personality just shine, he could turn in a moment and become rebellious and fight his obedience lessons tooth and nail.

He did get one over on all of us, however. While at PUPSI he quickly gained the reputation as the only dog we could not shampoo. He was a complete warrior in the tub. We had to introduce him to the wading pools the dogs played in and from there, the bathtub. Once again, by consistency and the human having the upper hand, Raleigh relaxed more and more each time, realizing there was nothing in the tub that would harm him. He got used to the water and the soap, but it was never his most favorite activity.

Raleigh is an example of a bright little dog with a lot of experience in getting his way. All dogs are cute in one way or another and if matched with an owner who lets it get away with anything, there is a problem. The problem is compounded when the dog is intelligent. As I've mentioned before, dogs do not forget anything. If a dog is allowed to build on an experience, dragging his owner down the street each and every time they go out, jumping from seat to seat in the car every time they go for a drive, jumping on anyone that comes in the front door, begging at the kitchen table…without any correction and consistency, the dog will continue getting his way.

SOME DOGS REQUIRE CONTINUAL WORK WITH OBEDIENCE WITH AN OWNER THAT HAS THE LAST WORD. MANY WILL PRESENT A CHALLENGE FOR MONTHS AND MAY LET THEIR NEGATIVE SIDE SLIP OUT FOR A LITTLE "TEST" EVEN YEARS DOWN THE ROAD.

YOU MUST WIN EVERY CONTEST.

HENLEY – A CHOCOLATE LAB THAT GOT IT RIGHT!

Years ago, when I first started PUPSI, a couple contacted me with a three month old Chocolate Lab named Henley. Labs are usually very easy to train at an early age and Henley proved no different. She did her breed proud.

The key to her perfect obedience was the diligence her owners invested in working with her. They followed my advice to the letter and worked with her consistently for three to four months after her basic program. Each time Henley came to board at PUPSI I bragged about her wonderful manners and the dedication her owners had with her. They truly did listen to everything I told them and taught them with their pup in basic obedience.

If more owners practiced what Henley's owners diligently did, the majority of problems would disappear with their pup. Karen and Todd, Henley's devoted owners, realized PUPSI had given Henley a wonderful base from which to continue to work from. Five simple commands and a few behavioral tips, including not jumping or puppy biting, was the base they worked from and built on with their dog. They were consistent in praising her and gave her a lifetime of learning in not too long of time. Once Henley learned the words and commands, all Karen and Todd had to do was practice with her. What a difference it made. The dog retained everything.

I have told and retold the story of Henley to many dog owners over the years. With just 20 minutes to ½ hour per day, after the basic obedience training, most owners would have a "near perfect" dog. All in all, that is not a great amount of time to commit to your pup and it will reward you for years to come.

DOGS LOVE TO LEARN. WITH PRAISE AND CONSISTENCY AND THAT "SOUND" OF LOVE IN YOUR VOICE, IT DOES NOT TAKE LONG TO GET THE RESULTS YOU WANT.

WORKMEN'S COMP, URGENT CARE!

In a meeting at PUPSI one day I started telling employees about funny moments at the kennel. Although not funny, I have been bit, more than once. It just seems to come with the territory. It also happens when you are least expecting it which, I guess is what makes it funny.

One morning I was getting ready to work with a new puppy that had come in for training. The dog was absolutely precious … any child would want a puppy like that one. It was a three month old female little Shih Tzu mix, a little ball of black and white fluff, with the cutest face. I was looking out the window and at the same time opening the kennel the dog was in. I nonchalantly put my hand inside the kennel door to pick up the pup and immediately heard that unmistakable sound, the growl, and was bitten so quickly I did not realize at first what had happened. I was shocked to have been bitten by such a cute puppy and embarrassed that I hadn't approached the puppy in a way that would have prevented the bite.

Another time, Trace and one of his friends had come to help at the kennel during a busy time. The boy with Trace had a baseball cap on and opened a kennel to get a collie mix in order to let it out so it could walk outside. Fortunately, I was close by just as the dog came lunging out of the kennel, fully intending to bite the boy. Moving about as swiftly as I could, I grabbed the dog as it jumped towards the boy, and was bitten five times before I could get it under control. We had not previously had a moment's trouble with the dog; he just did not like the baseball cap.

Often you can tell when you are about to be bit. The majority of the time it occurs when you try to get a dog out of a kennel and he doesn't want to come. One of the first lessons you learn in working with dogs, is to never corner a dog. Unfortunately, you learn this lesson by experience. A lot of dogs will go into a kennel just fine. It is when they make up their mind that they do not want to come out that you can have a problem. Many employees at PUPSI have had to learn the hard way especially if one of us were not right there to warn them not to grab the dog.

Another way you might get a warning is in training a dog. Some dogs dislike any sort of correction and will try to get the upper hand. We were working with a Rottweiler named Magnus a few years ago, teaching him basic obedience. Magnus was a beautiful example of the Rottweiler breed. He was very muscular and serious in appearance. He had a sweet side if he liked you, but was not one to be challenged. In training him, and giving a verbal command followed by a correction, the big boy decided he would try to do things his way and attempted to bite. These are times that you must be paying close attention to your student and how he or she may react. You have definitely got to be "thinking on your feet." Dogs move extremely quickly when they are ready to bite. You must be aware of their body language and be on your toes. Before Magnus could act on his aggression he found himself airborne at the end of the leash, as we had no other choice but to elevate Magnus to reinforce the command that was given the dog. In this position he could not bite and quickly calmed down. He challenged us more than once, as the dog was no pushover. With constant work and time, he learned to respect his commands and did not try to bite again.

When you have dogs playing together in a daycare situation you can not take your eyes off of them. Naturally, you know which ones have certain personalities and know what to watch for. We have dogs that come to daycare every day of the week, some that come a couple days per week and some we see every now and then. Dogs that arrive for boarding that are not part of the daycare group and all newcomers are always tested to see how well they will play. When you have been around dogs as long as we have, it only takes a minute to know if you have a "player" or not. Once you have your group, there is no guarantee that things will go smoothly. You must watch everyone; listen for growls and breakup dominant situations.

The fun comes when a fight begins and you find yourself in the middle of it. Unfortunately, you need to move as quickly as possible to restore order, getting the "bad guy" out of the situation (and sometimes it is more than one dog), where you find yourself literally pitching dogs out of the way as if you are pulling weeds and tossing them behind you. You honestly seem to gain some super human strength in such a situation as you do not want anyone to get hurt and you are moving as fast as you can. The adrenaline is certainly operating. However, once it is all over and things have calmed down, you often have a bite, maybe more, that you did or did not feel during the melee.

When dogs fight they are extremely focused on what is going on. Any time they are touched, be it on the shoulder, by the leg, on the tail, etc. they turn to bite what is touching them. It is not that they are personally attacking you; they feel the touch and turn to get it. Most kennel dog fights end with you or one of your staff on your way to the local urgent care facility to get cleaned up, as most dog bites can be nasty.

You must always remember that your dog can be dominant to some degree. If you do not pay attention to his dominance, you may quickly find yourself on the canine end of the stick with your dog operating as the owner. Never let your dog get away with growling at you, showing teeth, being food aggressive, not letting you remove an unacceptable item from his mouth, etc. Learn to correct your dog from an early age. If you have an older dog, let them know from the beginning that you are the owner. Never put your hands on your dog in an aggressive manner – no hitting, kicking, scruffing by the neck, kneeing in the chest. If you find you cannot correct a bad situation, seek the advice of a professional trainer.

Remember with all dogs, puppies and adults, tug of war games are not a good idea. Do not roll dogs over on their backs to establish dominance ... do not "growl" in their faces and stare them down. Simply use your voice and be serious in your tone when you are correcting your dog. Use a suitable collar, either nylon or prong, to give your dog a corrective jerk to get his attention, accompanied by your voice, if this is what it takes. With especially small dogs with tiny necks, you can even use a harness and lift the dog off the ground with the leash, letting him know you are serious.

HOUSEBREAKING 101

Over the years so many dogs of all types have come to PUPSI for housebreaking. We use the same system on all of the dogs unless the owner desires paper training or the latest, litter box training and the dog potty system. I always explain that housebreaking is used if the dog is expected to go to the bathroom outside where paper, litter training, and the potty system is for dogs that only go inside. So many owners try to get the dog to do both and the dog does not understand this. You have to pick one system and stick with it.

As I have said throughout this book, consistency is the key to everything. Accompany that with praise and you usually can get your pup to understand most anything you are trying to teach him. Housebreaking is no different. Where you run into a problem is with puppies from pet stores or environments where they learned to go to the bathroom inside, sleeping with it, playing with it and sometimes eating it. Most breeders who take over when the mother dog stops are ahead of the game when the pups go to a new home. You must keep the puppies as clean as possible and be ever cognizant about cleaning up the mess. Often older dogs have this problem, but it is more common with pups.

We have seen problems with all breeds, purebred and mutts. Some owners actually put up with it for over a year before they seek help. With older dogs it is often a request to get them housebroken when the owners decide they would like an outdoor dog to spend some time inside but are concerned that the dog will not know where to go to the bathroom or "ask" at the door to go outside. Most dogs that have spent the majority of their time outside are very easy to housebreak. Carpet is foreign to them and not their desired "spot". Trace's very latest dog, a golden retriever mix named Shooter was found wandering in the woods with his brother and taken to the SPCA. When he came to live with Trace he was very easy to housebreak as the great outdoors had been his spot for most of his very young life.

Whether you have a brand new pup or an older dog, if you are having a housebreaking problem there are a few steps you must follow to get on the right track. Once you have made the decision to get a dog, or if one arrives on your doorstep, you want to be prepared for your new family member.

The biggest reason there is a problem is odor control. I can take a perfectly housebroken dog who would not dream of going inside and if he "really" has to go, place a soiled piece of carpet in front of him next to a spot of grass. The majority of the time, the dog will choose the soiled, ever fragrant piece of carpet. If it smells right, the dog figures this is the place to eliminate.

If you do not treat all the areas of your home where the dog has soiled, you will have a problem. If you are in an apartment or home where a previous dog has lived, make sure you inspect the carpet and floors for any sign of earlier soiling. You can use a simple black light to pick up these areas and treat them with Nature's Miracle (the only product we recommend) to get rid of the odor. Nature's

Miracle is available at most pet stores. The best way to use it is to put it directly on the stain, cover it with a towel, blot it by stepping on the towel and leave it covered for a couple of days. You will be able to totally remove the stain and more importantly, the odor. You want to use this product wherever your dog had soiled. Wood floors, linoleum, furniture. It is so important to get the odor out.

Your next step is to have an area just for your dog or puppy. You should have a suitable size crate for the dog to rest in when you cannot be with him. Keep in mind, this is not forever. You must get your dog on the right track, follow up and do your part, be consistent and with time and age, your dog will get exactly where you want him to be on housebreaking. Crates do not equal cruelty. In fact, it is just the opposite. A crate is a safe place for your dog. It prevents young puppies from getting into things they can destroy or worse, things that can harm them. Even older dogs can be destructive. On the housebreaking end, a crate is a useful item and one that helps you greatly and makes your life easier in the housebreaking process. You cannot watch your dog continually while you are trying to achieve housebreaking. A crate is a necessary part of the process, unless you have a very small bathroom to keep the dog in but often that is too big. You cannot let your dog wander all over your house and be successful in housebreaking.

When you wake up in the morning, the first thing you do is address your needs. The dog comes next. Go and get your dog out of his crate and take him outside. Always use the same door and the same command. Whatever you want to say is fine. Just be consistent - always say the same thing. "Let's go outside", "wanna go potty", "hurry up", "do your business" are all adequate. Take the dog outside and STAY WITH HIM. You need to be able to shower him with praise when he goes to the bathroom. LOTS of "good boys" are what is needed when he does as expected. Take him back into the house and feed him. Allow 15 minutes for your dog to eat and drink water and then remove the food and water. Do not leave the water down. Your dog will not die from a lack of water. Remember, this is a housebreaking system. Consistency is crucial. If your dog did all that was expected of him when he was outside he should be fine while you are continuing on with your morning routine. If you are getting ready for work you need to know where he is, so keep him by you in the bedroom or put him in his crate with a toy or chew bone if you cannot be sure you can watch him. Before you leave for work offer him a few more minutes of outside time. When you leave, put him in his crate. No water. Be sure and leave a TV on or a radio. If you can place his crate by a window, even better. He can have some toys or a safe chewy. Remember to remove all collars from your dog anytime he is in the crate.

Depending on the age of your dog will determine how long he can stay in a crate. It is best if you can arrange to come home at lunch and you will need to do this if you have a very young puppy, four months or under. When you arrive back at home to take him out, enter the room where the crate is and be very calm. You do not want to get your dog so excited to see you that he wets all over the crate. Of course he will be happy to see you and will have heard you come in, but you need to be able to get him out of the crate and out the door, using the same words, same door as always. He should go to the bathroom rather quickly and once again he is ready to come in and play, eat if need be, have some water or even better, go for a walk. Just remember, dogs need to eat their meals after they have their walk. Never exercise your dog right after a meal. While you are trying to housebreak your dog you want to concentrate on the same door and the same purpose for going out into the yard. If you do not have a yard, you still want to be consistent in taking the dog to the area he is to use and bringing him back inside. Going for a walk is great but you don't want to confuse the dog when you are trying to housebreak him.

Be sure to put him back in his crate before you leave for the afternoon. Repeat the lunchtime process when you get home after work. If you are planning an evening walk, take him for his exercise before you give him dinner.

Spend some quality time with your dog in the evening and whenever you have time. Training a dog at the age of three months is the best time to begin. If you are working with a trainer, the evening is a great time to do your homework and the dog will enjoy it. Dogs love to spend time with their humans. This is another step in the ever important bonding process.

Be sure and take your dog back out to the bathroom before bedtime. While in the housebreaking process, cut all water off at 7 pm and do not let your dog drink until the next morning. In the summer months if you have spent some time outside later in the evening with your dog of course you must give him some water, but remember what goes in has to come out. So, allow the time to give the pup time to relieve himself before bed.

If the dog sleeps in a crate, which is a good idea while housebreaking, his most favorite place in the house will be your bedroom. If you place the crate in your bedroom put the dog to bed at the same time each evening. If you know that your dog's needs are all met and he protests in the crate, simply tell him "no" and leave the room. It will not take long for your dog to get used to the routine … as that is the key … stick to the routine.

If you have a young puppy and you have done everything you should in the day, do not be surprised if your pup wakes you up during the night. Most puppies can go about 5-6 hours and then need to go out. If the crate is not in your bedroom, please make sure it is somewhere in the house that allows you to hear your pup. If he has been asleep for a good while and you hear him starting to move around, by all means get up and take him out. He will be good for the rest of the night after this. If you stick to this routine you will get your dog housebroken.

If you are attempting to paper train or litter train your dog, this should only be done for the small breeds. Most small dogs dislike rain and snow and will refuse to go outside in inclement weather. The system is basically the same as housebreaking only you take the dog to the paper or the litter versus the outside area. One of the most convenient ways to use a litter box is to place it in the rear of the crate. Usually, when you wake up in the morning your pup will have already used the box. Take the dog out of the crate, feed and water, and place him back inside the crate for a few minutes. You will soon know how your little dog's system works and how long it will take him to go to the bathroom after he has had a meal. You will be able to figure out how long you can safely leave him out of the crate. You can do the same thing with the pads used for paper training as long as your dog doesn't shred it. Some puppies play with the paper pads. Be sure to keep the pads clean and consistently clean the litter box. If you are having a problem getting your pup to begin using the litter or the paper, get some of the pup's waste and place it on the pad or in the litter. You want the pup to understand what area he should be using.

If you are using pads and are against the crate, you must confine your dog in a small area with the pad. Do not cover the entire floor with the pads. You want the dog to go to the pad and use it. You can also do this with the litter box. I honestly feel the crate is the absolute best way to housetrain your dog, but with all the experience I have had with various dog owners, I realize not all people agree with the crate.

With the newest method, the dog potty system, all of the above steps are the same however you must show your dog his potty and take him to it each time you are trying to get him to relieve himself. Dog potty systems come in two sizes so they can be used for a large dog as well as a small one. Many people living in apartments or homes without yards opt for this new system. The potty comes with a type of canine grass that goes over a drain tray. You will need to purchase two pieces of this grass as every few days you need to wash one piece and allow it to dry before placing it back on the potty. Dogs can get accustomed to this system but it takes a bit more time and effort on your part. Additionally, do not purchase an inexpensive potty system as you get what you pay for. The more expensive ones are well built and the grass that comes with them will last and not fall apart.

Another crucial key to housebreaking your dog no matter what method you decide on, is to KNOW WHERE YOU DOG IS. I constantly preach this to my clients. For example, if you get up and take your dog outside first thing in the morning and he goes both ways things should be fine for a while. Depending on the age of your dog and the amount of food and water it takes in for breakfast, you should be able to trust your dog for a bit of time. However, you still need to know what he is doing. You cannot let your dog roam all over the house. This is not forever, it is just until your dog demonstrates the ability to begin going to the door to go out and not having any accidents in the house. If it is pouring down rain and you need to cook dinner and you know the dog needs to go out but isn't going for it, simply restrain the dog to a table leg in the kitchen and give it something to occupy its time and attention while you tend to your duties. If you are watching TV or working on your computer and you need to know what the dog is doing, restrain him to something nearby like a coffee table or chair leg. Again, give him something to occupy his time. Most dogs will NOT go to the bathroom when restrained. So, the likelihood of him relieving himself while you are right by him is slim.

The hardest dog I ever worked with in housebreaking was a Miniature Pincher named Bogey. His owner lived in a 3rd floor apartment and desperately needed help. MinPins can be a challenge to housebreak anyhow, and Bogey was no exception. I worked with him and let him go home when I felt he was ready. He did pretty well for a while then started marking his territory and regressing. Bogey returned to PUPSI and when he was ready to go a second time I made it clear that his owner had to keep him with her at all times when she was at home and in his crate when she was out. Bogey did great in the crate. His owner kept his leash tied to her while she went about her household duties and he finally learned that he couldn't get off in a corner somewhere so he began to whine each time he needed to go. That solved the problem as she was able to take him out and he would take care of business. After a few weeks of this type of consistency Bogey was completely housebroken and would go to the door each time he needed outside.

Speaking of the door, not all dogs will go to the door. If you are working with your dog and consistently going to the same door, using the same word and praising the dog for going, it still may be that your dog will never ask to go out. So many customers come to me asking me to teach their dog to ring a bell or bark to go out. With the 12 dogs that I currently own, only two will bark if they need to go out, one will go to the door and gaze outside and one will come and find me wherever I am to go out. Many dogs never indicate that they need to go out. This is why consistency and scheduling is so very important. This is why using the same door is critical in getting your dog to understand why he is going out of that door. It is up to you to watch for your dog's actions and expressions and realize what he needs to do. By the way, if your dog seems to be doing well with the same door and has an accident in front of that door, that is actually good news. It means your dog knows what the door is for. You just need to do your job and be paying attention to him when he goes to the door.

If you have worked with your dog and he seems to be getting the idea and you observe him backsliding and attempting to go to the bathroom in the house, you will need to know how to correct this. A shake can is an excellent tool that helps to reinforce your voice and comes in pretty handy in these situations. Get an aluminum can, wash it out and let it dry. Fill it 1/3rd full with pennies and tape the top. When you shake the can it makes a loud noise that will get your dog's attention. If you notice your dog circling or sniffing an area as if he is ready to go to the bathroom, pick the can up, shake it as you call his name accompanied with the word "no" and follow up with your command for going outside. (example: "Bailey, NO! Outside, outside"). Then you quickly take your dog out the door and even if he just dribbles, praise him for going.

If your dog can get through six weeks without an accident, you have won the housebreaking battle. After this time period, begin allowing him more freedom in the house but still be cognizant of your food and water scheduling and outside time. This is also the time that you put the litter box, puppy pad or dog potty where you want to permanently keep it and make sure the dog knows how to get to it from every room in the house. Don't forget the praise.

If you have litter trained, paper trained or used the dog potty system for your little dog, remember that they too enjoy a walk. It is good to let them experience the great outdoors as they can become very "barky" if not exposed to other dogs, humans, sounds etc. Many of the smaller breeds bark a lot anyhow, but it is always a good idea to help them become as social as possible. Remember that most little dogs that are litter or paper trained do not go to the bathroom outside.

The oldest dog we ever housebroke was a seven year old poodle. The owner simply got tired of the dog going to the bathroom in her downtown Raleigh home. Actually, the system we use worked extremely well and the dog wasn't at PUPSI very long before he caught on. We simply started him in a small space, treating him like an 8 week old puppy, scheduling his food and water and introducing him to the outside, accompanying him each time and praising him for relieving himself. As he progressed, he was given more space inside to sleep and play in but we continued to keep him on a schedule and praise him each time he went outside. His last step in his progression was to leave him in one of our rooms with a bed and toy and supervise him. Once he completed that test and kept the room clean, he was ready to go home. Most toy and miniature poodles are pretty easy to deal with. The standard poodle can be a challenge. This older miniature was very smart and it took a short time for him to understand that he could go to the bathroom outside. You can teach an old dog new tricks.

Another little dog came to me with diaper rash and diapers. The woman's husband had threatened to get rid of the dog because it could not be housebroken. We worked with this little dog by removing the diaper, which also got rid of the rash, and letting it stay in a small exercise pen outside each time we took her out. I often explain to people that do not have fenced in yards that you can purchase an exercise pen at most pet stores and the pen is a great way to keep your dog housebroken and give you some time to yourself. Exercise pens come in three different heights and all conveniently fold down upon themselves for easy carrying and set up. They have ground stakes to keep them from blowing over and offer plenty of room. Your dog will remain safe in the pen and can go about its business while you are able to go back inside for a few minutes until you are ready to bring the dog back in.

Additionally, you can tell each time your dog has relieved itself because the area is small enough to allow you to keep it clean and be able to see the evidence left by the dog. They are great for cold days, rainy days and times when you know the dog has to go and you have something else you must do. The pen worked so well for the woman that she purchased one and was able to keep her dog. I received the nicest thank you note from her and her amazed husband.

Naturally, we want everyone to be able to keep their dog. People that come to PUPSI are willing to invest the time and money into helping their dog. It is very gratifying to be able to see everyone happy with the new family member.

Housebreaking, paper training, litter box training, and the dog potty system can take a bit of time. But, if you follow the rules of odor control, food and water scheduling, same door, same word, lots of praise and knowing where you dog is, it can be achieved. The time it takes depends on the early days of the pup's life, the age of your dog, the habits it has picked up and the time you are willing to put into it. Before you know it, your young dog has grown up and soiled carpet, floors or furniture is a distant memory. Remember, older dogs can catch on too.

One more quick story before I end this lecture on housebreaking. A lady had a Basset Hound puppy that she wanted housebroken. The dog did well and the day before she came to pick her up she called to tell me she had gone through a couple of bottles of Nature's Miracle treating her house but was going to give it one more shot. She bought a black light and found 52 more spots where her puppy had eliminated! Odor control is a major step in achieving the results you are looking for in housebreaking OR paper training, litter box or dog potty.

MY DOG IS REALLY SMART ... HE JUST DOESN'T FEEL LIKE DOING THOSE COMMANDS!

Sometimes we run into a client who has taken her dog through previous dog training classes or has trained the dog on her own who insists she only needs help in one or two areas and that the dog is really well trained.

Our first reaction is to ask what she would like us to do. Many times we try to talk these people out of our training the dog because we know from experience what it means when an owner insists their dog is "well trained." They usually mean they want the dog to learn tricks versus having dog training. We usually explain that we don't have the time to do tricks but we can tell them how to do it at home. It also means the dog is really not well trained at all.

Usually when we get these dogs enrolled for training, the first day we often discover that the dog is dominant, and may already know one command, but is certainly not a master at it or anything else. These dogs are usually bad jumpers and nippers and often bark at you to get your attention, trying to distract you from speaking to anyone else. I had one lady who called with a Jack Russell Terrier who would jump on her and pull the clip out of her hair each and every time she got on the phone. We cured this problem by demonstrating the corrective jerk. Jack Russell's have thick little necks and are very hardy dogs. Once we convinced her that her dog could tolerate a correction and definitely needed one, her dominating dog problem ended. She had to assume the role of owner and correct the dog by keeping it on a leash with a sturdy nylon collar so she was able to grab the leash and jerk the dog whenever he resumed his jumping up, biting, getting her hair clip role. It took less than a week for the problem to end and everyone, including the Jack Russell was happy.

Training your dog should be as common as feeding your dog. It is necessary. You and everyone else in your life will enjoy your dog so much more if she understands the basics. The majority of the time all that is needed is the basics. On leash, heel, sit, stay, down, come, no jumping and no puppy biting. If you can get these under both of your belts you are far ahead of the game.

I have often talked about a chocolate lab named Henley to many of my clients. When she came to me for training at the age of three months she was a typical lab puppy, very cute and ready to learn. She sailed through the basic obedience course and her owners did their job. They consistently worked with Henley for a few months while she was a puppy and then it was done. Henley continued to come to PUPSI whenever her owners went out of town and she was always the most perfect boarder, a wonderfully socialized dog, and just great to have around. Any family would be proud of her. The point being that it did not take "forever" to get the dog this way. Patience and consistency are the basics and her owners followed through 100%. Additionally, they didn't wait until the dog was grown and had already gotten away with bad habits before they had her trained.

If you have a problem with your dog or simply a dog that does things her way and you are having a difficult time communicating with it, get yourself enrolled in some dog training class. There is nothing like sound, professional advice and a small amount of time on your part to create a well trained, enjoyable family member. Your dog will have so much more respect for you and life will be a lot easier.

BEAR, BUDDY AND HARRY

Bear is a cute, dark gray, long haired chow something mix. Buddy is a red, short haired pit bull mix. Harry is a tall, black, lab mix. All three of these dogs came to PUPSI with the same problem. All three were very shy of people and needed socialization with humans and canines alike. Each of their owners wanted their dog to be more relaxed in general.

When a dog exhibits shy behavior he has very wary looking eyes. He watches people constantly. He does not typically like someone to walk up behind him and may turn suddenly and cower down. These dogs exhibit behavior very similar to fear biters, without the bite. For many reasons, they have become very shy of people. Since dogs never forget anything negative from the time they open their eyes and because they cannot tell us what is wrong, we need to try and figure out what has made them this way. They are very easy to spot as their eyes seem to tell the story. Often, they are very wide eyed and very nervous.

Never ones to turn anyone away with a dog problem, the staff at PUPSI decided to take each one on. We always tell an owner that we cannot guarantee their dog will decide to trust people and to like other dogs but we will give it our best shot. Often, as in the case of leash aggression, it is not the dog with the problem, but that of a nervous owner. Sometimes, especially with an older dog, you cannot turn it around and the owner ends up with a dog that is not social with other dogs or trusting with people. Additionally, you cannot fight genetics and you must study the breed you are working with and realize some very basic characteristics often stay in place, no matter how well the puppy is raised.

Bear, Buddy and Harry have each come a long way at PUPSI. Not only have they learned to trust humans but are now fine with other dogs. It took a lot of patience and a staff knowledgeable in watching and waiting to see how each dog reacted with other dogs. It took each person at PUPSI who came in contact with each dog a lot of time to show each dog that they could be trusted and there was nothing to be afraid of. In circumstances like this, everyone must work together to be easy with the dog, not making any quick moves or loud noises. The last thing you want to do is startle the dog. We want to take steps forward not backward. All of the techniques, being calm, being patient, reassuring, consistent, took a bit of time, but today all three run through the doors at PUPSI and cannot wait to get outside to the playground. Each one can now be petted nonchalantly and bathed easily with nothing to fear. Earning a dog's trust is not a difficult thing if you are calm, soft spoken and reassuring to them that they will be just fine. To this day, at drop off time in the morning, they each still give a look back at their owners as if to say, "this is OK, right?" and each of their owners have done an especially fine job in allowing the PUPSI staff to work with the dogs, trusting in our knowledge and taking our advice.

Those are three success stories. Be reminded once more that when you are seeking dog daycare for your dog, or any kind of dog care, you must do your homework and make sure the staff handling your dog is ever present in any group situation.

You should feel comfortable when leaving your dog in their care for any reason, training, boarding, grooming or daycare, that the facility is manned with real "dog people," able to handle any situation. Talk to the people that are taking care of your dog. It's easy to tell who has experience and who doesn't. It is not difficult to determine if a person likes your dog. When you pick your dog up, a good indicator is how the dog acts around the personnel at the kennel. With the passing of each day it will not be a challenge in most cases to figure out if your dog is comfortable at the kennel you have chosen.

Never settle on a facility that only uses cameras to supervise the dogs in their care. Real walking, talking, dog people should be with your dog any time he is around other dogs. A camera cannot break up a fight.

Dog training "degrees" are not necessary. Check out the facility online, see what other people have to say about the place. When you are considering a certain place, visit it. The friendliness and warmth of the staff says a lot. Cleanliness is another very important factor. Watch other dogs with the staff. Remember, once you choose a place, give them a chance. If you dog seems tired when you pick him up, do not panic. Tired is usually good.

One of the biggest mistakes owners make is wondering why their dog is tired and not interested in a big meal, so they rush their dog to the vet, only to find out that he is just fine. Any new situation is a bit stressful on a dog, but there is good stress and bad stress. Good facilities understand that and will ease your dog into the new situation and be ever watchful for any bad stress. Good facilities will tell you how you dog did that day with the other dogs and staff. Most people that find a good kennel continue to come back. PUPSI has clients that have brought their dogs to them for years. It is not unusual for them to bring their new puppy to us once they add another to the family or, sadly when they lose their buddy and get a new one. You want a facility that has that type of reputation.

SPEAKING OF THAT TRUSTING THING...

I constantly remind people that dogs do not forget anything negative from the time they open their eyes. Throughout their lives they will remember any negative thing, some can be overcome, and some cannot.

Loud noises can startle young dogs. With time and careful introduction of certain sounds and noises, such as traffic, construction, etc. you can be successful in reversing the negative effect these noises have had in the past on a dog. The more you take a dog out in public by walking and on car rides, the better conditioned the dog will become to all sorts of noises.

Many puppies have a hard time walking down a public sidewalk in the beginning. Cars and trucks passing by startle them and the wind the vehicles create makes them jump to one side of the car or crouch down. The more and more you subject the pup to the walks and to rides in the car, the easier and quicker he will get used to it. We have had puppies at PUPSI that are so afraid of the outside world we have to take them to downtown Cary and actually sit on a bench with them to get them accustomed to traffic noises, construction sounds and police sirens. With time and patience and constant reassurance to the dog that all is well, by petting and talking to him, you can usually turn it around.

As trainers we can tell if a dog is hand shy. This means that when you go to pet the dog or even give a command such as "stay" where you hold your hand palm side up towards the dog, the dog will flinch, possibly wince and could even whine. The dog will almost always show his submissive side and crouch towards the floor. Usually this indicates that the dog has been hit with a hand, kicked with a foot, or had something thrown at it.

Years ago I worked with a young Rottweiler who was very hand shy. The woman who brought him to me told me that the dog had started showing teeth and growling whenever she approached it or tried to pet it.

The owner drove up on the second day of training with me and jumped out of her car exclaiming, "Mary, you're petting him!" She was so shocked to see me standing on the sidewalk nonchalantly stroking the dog's head. It had taken me just two days to get him to trust me. Of course I did not start out by trying to pet the dog. Instead, I worked with him and used my hand under his chin to praise and pet him. I was able to move my hand to the more normal petting fashion on the second day of training because the dog had experienced nothing negative from working with me. The owners were not abusive people. They had simply gotten the wrong advice from a trainer who had worked with the dog prior to me. The trainer had told them to scruff the dog by the neck whenever he did anything wrong; jumped on them, grabbed their hand as if to nip, would not release a toy or if the dog had something he shouldn't.

Kneeing in the chest, scruffing the neck and rolling dogs over on their backs are three things I totally disagree with in training a dog. These include spraying the dog in the face with bug spray or

Listerine and placing leashes around their muzzles. Would you kick a child in the chest if they jumped on you? How about spraying the child in the face with Listerine if she yelled too loud?

Dogs ask nothing of us. In my way of thinking they don't get enough of our time and attention for all that they give to us. They are totally loyal, never complaining, always happy to be with us. Many are our protectors. Many have had a hard beginning in life: discarded like waste. Some have endured pain, been run over by cars, shot, and dropped off in the middle of nowhere. Yet, given a chance, many of these dogs can overcome all of that and give someone their love and loyalty.

I didn't perform any magic on the Rottweiler. He had learned that his owner's hands meant one thing … that he would be grabbed by the neck and shook and told "no!" When he got old enough he decided to protest this action by his owners and learned if he showed his teeth and growled they would back off. After explaining all of this to them and telling them to start all over again with their dog, going slowly, they were able to rebuild the trust in their dog that they had lost.

Often even good owners just get a lot of bad advice.

CHASING CARS

Some dogs are very attracted to chasing cars, bicycles, roller blades, or roller skates. While the latter three probably do not pose as much of a danger as an automobile, dogs should be discouraged from chasing anything. It is not a difficult thing to do but once again takes time and consistency.

Shetland Sheepdogs, or Shelties as they are normally referred to, are very likely to be car chasers. We have had quite a few in for training at PUPSI that include chasing on their list of "what needs to be worked on." Shelties are alert little dogs and the noise of the oncoming car seems to attract them.

The dog needs to be taught a few first steps in basic obedience prior to working with it on car chasing. He should know sit, no and stay. Once the dog has a good command of these three basics, he is ready to be worked on with his attraction to cars. You must have a good collar, either a prong or nylon choker and a good leash. If you are using the prong, make sure all of the prongs are correctly attached to each other. It is extremely important that you have purchased a high end prong collar, no matter what command you are teaching. Nylon chokers should be in good shape with no tears. If the dog is really small, as some Shelties are, you may choose to use a harness, but make sure it fits correctly: It should be tight all around his body with a good connector and no torn places.

Take the dog to the edge of the street, end of the driveway, on a sidewalk, or wherever cars are likely to go by. As the car approaches and you see him perk up, tell him to sit. As the car gets closer, use the command "no" and "stay". If he jumps up as the car passes you must be ready to give him the corrective jerk and make him sit again. Use a firm "no" so he will gradually understand that this is something he cannot do. It may take a few days but if you are consistent the dog will get the idea.

If he seems very stubborn and tries to run across your lawn after a car you can use a 15 – 20 foot lead attached to his collar. Once you have worked with him up close to the street you will need to make sure he will obey you even if he is away from the street but still noticing the traffic. Measure the distance from a place in your yard to the edge of the street. Use a long lead and attach it to the dogs collar. Hang around in the yard with the dog, acting as if you are not paying much attention to him. When you hear an oncoming car coming close enough grab the lead if he decides to run after it. If he begins to run, give the command, "(dog's name), no…stay" and be prepared to jerk him away from the street if he does not stop. You want him to get almost to the end of the leash so you can really give him a correction and he will begin to realize that he isn't going to win.

This command can take some time in teaching, but it is an all important one if you have a car chaser. In a family with a dog like this everyone must always pay close attention to opening doors that lead out onto a street. It only takes a moment and your buddy can end up under a car. If you feel like you have not mastered the command, take your dog to a trainer who can consistently work with the dog. It is important to get the dog to forget all about cars.

DIGGING HOLES

Oh the woes of the homeowner with the landscaped yard and the dirt digging, mud loving dog. At least 60% of the clients that come to PUPSI ask what can be done about the dog digging up their yard. They spend hours planting and it only takes a moment for a dog to destroy their day's work.

Dogs can go for weeks or months on end and not touch anything in the yard. Then, all of a sudden you can look out your window and find a hole big enough to bury a car in! Better yet, when it rains the hole is like a small swimming pool: filled with mud.

Nothing is more aggravating then to open your door to a dog standing on your deck that is covered in mud. It's especially good if it's about 10 pm in the evening, you've had your bath and are ready for bed, and now you get to somehow "bathe" the dog before you can have any thoughts of retiring. If it's a big dog, forget about retiring, because you will need to mop the floor as well as any furniture he touches or shakes on as he passes by on his way to the bath. Of course, if it is freezing cold outside, an outside hose bath is obsolete.

We have an Alaskan Malamute that we refer to as the eternal two year old. We had to pour concrete in our back yard to get rid of the mud. If dirt or grass was still there, I promise you, she would be digging it up and her paws and nose would be covered in it. She is now eight years old!

The easiest way to begin to work on the problem is to catch the dog while he is digging. If you can scare your dog you can almost be sure of winning at the digging game. Sneaking up on a dog is pretty impossible to do, so you must be quick.

If your dog is digging in the yard, get a bag of cheap balloons from the drugstore. Blow up a couple, sneak up behind the dog and pop them as close as possible to him. If this inexpensive trick works, it's over. He will stop. You must, however, follow this up with more balloons for a few days. Once you have succeeded in scaring him with the noise, you then need to blow up enough balloons to surround the hole. Secure them in the ground around the hole and leave it like that for a week or so. The same trick can be used for getting in trashcans. You must catch the dog in the trash. Sneak up and pop a balloon as close to his head as possible. Once again, if it scares him you have won. This trick will not work however, if the dog is not scared when the balloon is popped. If successful, blow up a few balloons and place them in the top and around the trash can and leave them for a few days.

Mousetraps are another deterrent. Purchase the wooden, small, inexpensive ones. You may feel like you are after a rat, but this is your dog! Small, mouse size is what you are looking for. Set the traps around the trash can, in it and on top. If your dog sniffs around and begins to disturb the trash, all of the traps will go off at once and he will normally run away. Once again, you won. You can use the small mousetraps around holes in the yard too. (With our Alaskan Malamute, Jazz, you would be a total failure. She is not afraid of anything…a gun could go off by her head and she would just look around. The only thing I know that she does not care for is a moth and it would be difficult to get enough of them to scare her out of any mud hole or trash can!)

If your dog is digging in the same spot in the yard all the time you will need to bury a garden hose, face up. Watch for him to begin his digging routine and when he gets into it, turn on the hose full blast. It doesn't take much imagination to understand why this trick works. It makes a muddy mess, but it does work.

Often you will have to repair the hole with fresh dirt and fence it in until new grass has grown. The surprise of the water usually scares the dog and they will usually not return to that area.

The most extreme way to fix the problem, if you have a very stubborn dog who won't submit, is to purchase an electric fence from a local home improvement store or a shock collar. Neither one is inhumane, but you need to know how they work. The fence can be purchased rather inexpensively and you can install it. One of the most popular brands is Fido Fence. This is NOT invisible fence; this is actually a wire that you can see. You can run it around the hole(s) in your yard and when the dog goes to dig and touches it, he will be shocked. It will not take any time at all before the dog is leaving all of the holes alone.

If you purchase a shock collar that your dog actually wears, remember that you get what you pay for. Don't purchase the low end collar and don't purchase the most expensive. A good, middle of the road brand is fine. The collar comes with a hand held device that you operate. Place it on your dog and observe him closely. Once he goes anywhere near the hole(s), give him a verbal correction, such as "Barney, no" followed with a quick shock if he ignores your warning. Again, this method is the most costly and most extreme, but it will get the job done. In either case the dog will not think you are doing anything to him. He will think it is the hole!

NOT THE VETERINARIAN!

Just the other day a client of ours requested something we've never been asked to do before. Her dog was at the vet to have some blood work done and would not cooperate. No matter what they tried, nor how many attempts they made to restrain the dog, it was wasted effort. The client left the vet's office and requested that WE take her dog to the vet. The visit had ended with the dog lunging at one of the vet techs and snapping at her face.

This is a typical case of a dog that is controlling the owner as well as everyone else around it. I cannot stress how important it is to start immediately when you buy, adopt, or find your new family member, by working on being the owner and controlling your dog. You do not need to resort to any type of abuse or yelling. Teach the dog what you want him to learn. Praise and consistency comes through once more. Dogs know when you are happy with them and they love to please. In the case of the client's dog and the vet, the dog was very scared, probably from a past situation. We were able to go over, walk the dog around outside the vet's office for a bit, then slowly and easily help keep him calm while they drew blood. This is not always the case. Remember, once a dog is exposed to a negative situation it does not forget. The dog was a regular at PUPSI and very accustomed to all of us. He had never experienced anything negative at PUPSI and it was one of his favorite places to be. Often dogs that have been terrified at a veterinarian's office remain that way. Unfortunately, many vets have to resort to tranquilizing the dog with something so simple as a nail trim.

One of the most important things you can do with your new family member no matter what the age of the dog, is to prepare her for a trip to the vet. While you are playing with and petting her, make it a routine every few days to look in her eyes, poke gently in her ears with your fingers, open her mouth, feel her sides and belly. Every couple of weeks trim her nails. Nail clipping is not difficult if you do the job right each time. When you look at a dog's nail you can see white and pink. The pink area is the area to avoid, that is where the actual blood is located and if you cut into it you will have a sore paw and a bleeding one. Purchase some good nail clippers and begin clipping her nails as soon as you get her. Pay attention to the dew claw on the front legs, it can grow long relatively quick and curl into her leg. Only a few breeds have rear dew claws and if your dog has these, they will need to be clipped also. Dark or black nails need to be trimmed carefully as you cannot see the pink area. You can also purchase a dremmel at the local hardware store and begin using it on the nails. While the motor does make noise, if you start early in your dogs life and have the dremmel on a lower speed, your dog should be just fine. You may need someone to help you hold you dog, but that is alright. Dremmel's do a great job and actually smooth out and round the nail.

Begin by just taking off a bit and getting the sharp point down. If your dog immediately protests you must be extremely careful not to let her pull her leg backwards as you are clipping. You do not want to pull out a nail or rip it. Often, with the help of another person you can calm the dog down and finish the job. If you have a dog that is a real battle, let a veterinarian do the job. Dogs that have experienced a problem with nail clippings in the past are usually the ones that are the tough ones to do their nails.

The reason you want to do all of these things with your dog is so your trip to the veterinarian will be a good one, absent of any fear or nervousness. You want your dog to enjoy going to the vet, just as you want her to ride in the car and be social. Starting early at home is a great way to make trips to the vets uneventful.

PACK MENTALITY

If you are in a household with more than one pet, the simple rule is let them work it out. With time, cats will live with dogs and dogs will live with other dogs. I've seen households with dogs, cats and bunny rabbits. I've seen lizards and dogs, spider monkeys and dogs. The pot bellied pig seems to get along fine with all animals. Once again, it is the humans that need to relax.

My big male Alaskan Malamute, Cuda is all dog and 100% male. He does not like other dogs and is extremely protective of me. On any given day while out walking, the fur will go up on his back whenever he sees another dog. Little dogs don't cause this reaction but any sizeable dog does. He will watch the dog closely and we will detour around it, letting the other owner know he is not friendly towards other canines. If the other dog makes any type of aggressive move, Cuda will let him know with all teeth showing that he is not to take another step.

When we first brought our female Malamute Jazz into the home, she was about three months old. We knew we would have to watch them closely. The fact that she was a female meant nothing. Things progressed well for about a week until one evening she got too close to him in the kitchen and he turned and bit her. Of course, we were right there and reprimanded him and found she was just scared, not hurt. Scaring her into submission was what he wanted to accomplish and to this day she respects him. Every now and then she will growl at him if she is sleeping and doesn't want to move, but nothing more has ever come of that.

Yuki was the second Malamute we introduced to Cuda. She was three months old and a female. He was just as unhappy at her arrival as he had been with Jazz. Yuki stayed in the kitchen in an exercise pen during the day when we couldn't be in the same room with her. One afternoon, something came up and we had to run out of the house and thought she would be just fine in the kitchen for less than an hour. Leaving her in the exercise pen was a mistake. Apparently Yuki realized we were gone and jumped against the pen until she was free. When we arrived back home, the pen was turned over and empty and Cuda greeted us with his ears down. Normally when he does this we know someone has chewed something up, gone to the bathroom on a rug, gotten sick, or whatever. Cuda always lets us know if something wasn't quite right. I wish I could hear him talk to the girls, I'm sure he would say something like: "You two are in for it now."

We searched the house for Yuki and found her upstairs under the bed. She seemed just fine and we decided she had gotten out of the pen and Cuda had probably scared her and she ran. Later in the evening we had her on the bed petting her and felt something sticky and moist. She had a hole in her head. The hole was the perfect size of a large canine tooth. Cuda had obviously grabbed her and bitten her. It was as if he had broken right through her scalp. With a series of antibiotics and making sure we kept the wound clean, Yuki healed just fine. It took quite a while however, for her to be comfortable around Cuda which again is what he wanted.

As with Jazz all of that changed when each female came into heat. When both Jazz and Yuki came into our household, Cuda only recognized them as inferior members of the house. He was not aware of or cared about their sex. When each one went through her first heat cycle, the whole picture changed. While Cuda was still the dominant dog he found a new interest in each of them and was far more accepting of them.

Today, the three of them coexist just fine. Bones and toys are no problem and Cuda is a complete gentleman. Both females know he is the boss and, except for an occasional growl, life with the three of them is just fine.

Oddly enough, when I brought Cuda into the household as a younger dog, two older males lived here. Instead of asserting his dominance, he respected their domain, and although he quickly took over top position, he was never aggressive to either one of the males. It was as if he was a guest in their home at first who gradually took over.

We have all read stories or seen documentaries on wolves and how they exist with a very definite pack structure. It is not much different in a household with multiple pets. In their world, someone is going to be dominant. As owners we must be dominant over our animals, but if you have more than one pet, you will soon see that one is the most dominant over the others.

We get many requests from clients at PUPSI about solving their problem of multiple pets in the home. In a few instances we have had to help clients set up harsh rules when one animal will not accept another's presence. Certainly no one wants to see their pet hurt. Trips to the vet to patch up ears and serious bites are very costly.

Most of the time when we tell clients how to correct behavior in animals sharing a household it is to just give the situation some time, the animals work it all out. It's very difficult to live in a home where you have to keep the animals apart but I have also seen households that do this. Each animal has its own room and gets to spend quality time on a schedule with its owners. More than likely, these are owners who are too afraid to "risk" letting the animals work it all out.

As an owner in control of any situation, as time progresses most animals will submit and listen to your corrections. With the simple tone of your voice any animal in your household will know if you are displeased. Each pet that comes into your household must be given the same chance and worked with with patience, bonding, respect and most importantly, consistency. Patience and consistency always pay off in the long run.

Jazz

Wonderful Cuda

At the Outer Banks NC with Cuda and Jazz

BOREDOM

Dogs can and do get bored. If you combine this with an active breed, be prepared for chewed furniture, destroyed carpets, ruined landscaping and lots of barking. Bored dogs are forever juveniles… they never seem to grow up. Keep in mind that dogs are omnivores. They will eat everything and often they do!

The easiest answer to boredom is exercise. If you can tire your dog out each day his bad habits will quickly disappear and he will use his spare time to rest.

Take the case of our dear BJ, a 110 lb. Alaskan Malamute/Siberian Husky mix that I just had to rescue from the flea market. BJ was by far the most destructive dog I have ever owned. He even topped my shepherd Rainbow, and she ate couches! BJ is the original no fear dog. The energy of the Siberian Husky made up most of his genes and it took him a good three years plus to mature. He ate couch cushions and chair pillows by the dozen. He scratched the kitchen table as if it were nothing, always begging for food. (My mother lived with us when BJ was young and she adored him. Every time she sat down for a meal, he would get part of it.) The moment he was left alone everything was fair game. He could destroy an item in no time, and was extremely quiet while shredding things.

The outside world was his paradise. BJ has killed and eaten squirrels and birds. He has killed a snake and a possum, choosing not to eat either. He loved to stalk his prey like a cat. Heaven forbid the times he would get past my mother out the front door. The neighborhood was put on alert until he was retrieved, as each cat and every dog were instantly in his sights.

In 1995, during Hurricane Fran in North Carolina, there were four dogs living in the house. In the middle of the night they wanted to go outside. All that we had heard of the hurricane was wind noise and it did not sound too bad. I turned on the outside lights and let the dogs out. A few minutes later when I opened the door to let them in, only three returned. Of course BJ was the one missing in action. Not knowing why he wasn't answering my call, I turned on the flood lights and realized our back fence was gone in three different sections. I went outside in the wind and rain and BJ raced by having the time of his life. The only way we got him to come in was to start the car. He always loved going for a ride. He finally jumped in the car. I have never known that dog to be afraid of anything.

The only solution for putting an end to his escapades indoors and out was to run his legs off. Fortunately, I love to run, so it was not a problem. BJ soon became so conditioned to our daily routine that he looked forward to it. He could run in any temperature, and we did. However, it still took time and age to get him to relax.

Our dear BJ passed away on January 24, 2007. He was just shy of 14 and his running days were only in his dreams at that point of his life. He lived in the office at PUPSI but got very arthritic and had a terrible time getting around. During the last few weeks of his life he seemed to decline very quickly. He would still eat, but spent most of the time sleeping. I think he would still dream and recall some of the best days of his life, chasing squirrels, catching a bird, treeing a cat. Perhaps every now and then those memories of Hurricane Fran came into his mind.

BJ will always be a wonderful memory in our lives. I have never known another dog to be as completely fearless as he was. His ashes sit in my living room in a plain black urn but someday I plan to have a special urn made for him, emphasizing his carefree manner and his no fear attitude.

BARKING

Why do dogs bark? There are many reasons.

Often dogs bark because they are so very happy to see you. Sometimes it is as if they are almost singing. Siberian Huskies and Alaskan Malamutes tend to howl in delight when they are happy to see you. They also howl at passing emergency sirens.

Wolves bark to alert their pack of danger. Dogs bark for the same reason. Many breeds and mixes are extremely protective of their human family and will alert them if something does not seem quite right.

Lots of dogs bark when they are playing with humans or with each other. Many will emit harmless growls. When dogs wrestle with each other there is usually some barking involved.

Outgoing dogs are usually very energetic and can be a handful but are also great for owners who want an active dog. These are the ones you see who never seem to tire, like the Eveready Battery Rabbit … they keep going and going. These types seem to bark for almost any reason, but their bark is usually an extension of their hyperactivity.

Aggressive dogs have a very distinct bark. It is easy to tell the difference in a dog that is barking for positive reasons and a dog that is growling and barking aggressively.

On the other side of the coin, there are dogs that bark to get your attention. These dogs fall into the category of those whose owners have not taken control. We have had many students at PUPSI with the barking to annoy and get attention problem. Most will bark at us when we are working with them on their various commands. If the dog is one that has really taken charge at home, the barking will begin on the very first training day. We immediately correct it and get the owner to understand that barking for attention is not acceptable. I have had many clients bring dogs in who say they cannot talk on the phone, sit on the couch and watch TV, read a book, etc. without their dog continuously barking at them. Unfortunately, most owners have given in to the dog by getting up and playing with the dog, taking it for a walk and forgetting all about their own lives. The problem is not difficult to correct IF we can convince the owner to take over.

A dog that barks, growls and shows teeth after given a command is a dog that must be reckoned with immediately. This is never acceptable. Often we hear the complaint that a dog will not get off an owner's bed or couch. When the owner tries to get the dog down he retaliates by growling and showing teeth. Again, this is a problem that an obedience trainer can fix if the owner is unwilling to try and is actually afraid of the dog. In this case, the dog is almost in complete control. Do not wait to get help.

Your dog should never growl, show teeth or try to bite you in any situation. It is true that any dog will attempt to bite if it is physically hurt, but in normal situations a dog that tries to bite you is a dog that has taken over or is planning on it.

From the time you get your dog begin to be the owner. If you experience any of the problems above, you will need to take over and correct them immediately. Chances are, if you always correct negative barking, growling, and showing teeth, you will never get to the point of being afraid of your dog. Once again, you must win in each situation. If your dog is allowed on the sofa then you can never ask him to get down. However, if you do not desire him to be on the sofa ever, you must stick to it and not allow it. If your dog hops up on the couch you need to get him down at once. If you approach and he begins to growl use your serious voice and tell him no and place him on the floor. If your concern is that he may bite, get his leash and collar, place it on him and use it to get him off the couch. You must make him realize that you will not allow his getting on the furniture.

If your dog is a barker you will need to correct this behavior as well. Simply use your voice, tell him no and ask him to do something for you. For example, correct him, make him lie down and give him a chew stick or something that belongs to him and walk away. Often ignoring the problem stops it. If you are on the phone and the barking begins, walk over, place his leash and collar on him, give him a corrective jerk accompanied with a stern no, and get back to your conversation. If you give him something he enjoys in any negative situation with a positive remark and a pet on the head, most dogs will eventually prefer the positive treatment over the negative. You must establish the ground rules and use the same type of correction each time. The dog will soon learn what is and what is not allowed.

THE "IN CHARGE" DOG

If you find that you have a dominant dog that wants to be in charge, you will need to work with him with patience. You will need to win in every situation no matter how long it takes you. If you have a dog that refuses to take a command and ends up growling or barking at you, you must be prepared to correct the dog and make him do the command, no matter how long it takes. Once you give in and walk away the dog has won. Most dogs with this temperament are very smart and will remember that you lost on that command. They will build on your loss if they can get away with it.

For example, if you are working with you dog on the "sit" command and he refuses to do it, and you lose patience and walk into the house, it will be even harder to get the dog to sit the next time you begin working on it. Patience is something you must be armed heavily with. Never hit or kick your dog into submission. A dog learns nothing from this. You can certainly use your voice and we urge you to do this in all dog training. Screaming is not a good option as it wears you out a lot sooner than the dog. It accomplishes nothing. It may raise your blood pressure but most dogs just look at you like you are the one that has lost it …and you are.

You must take the time to show the "in charge" dog what you want. By using the correct collar and a serious tone of voice and showing him the command, with time you will win. The dog with this challenging personality will end up showering you with respect and usually turns out to be a great dog with a lot of intelligence. Once again, your tone of voice and a quick jerk on the collar with your leash is the best first step to establishing your ground. You must get your dogs attention and let him know you plan on winning, no matter what. Do not lose control. Do not lose your patience. Take the time to teach your dog what you want. Don't forget to praise, praise, praise once your dog does what you ask.

SHY GUYS

Often the little pup you pick out of the litter that hangs at the back of the crowd and you feel sorry for, turns out to be very submissive. Dogs that have been abused can be very shy and very untrusting. Genetics play a role in this trait. A puppy can easily take on the submissiveness of its mother, father or other ancestor if that trait is in the line. Patience certainly will be needed in any of these cases.

We have had many dogs at PUPSI that are scared of their own shadow. These dogs take a lot of time in training. Socialization is a big part of their day at the kennel. Many are so scared of daily common noises. A police siren, a construction truck, a garbage truck, a bicycle, roller skates – any and all of these can scare a submissive dog. I've worked with dogs that will literally run in the opposite direction if a person walks by. They try to get under anything that's convenient in order to hide,

Sitting on a park bench by a busy road is one of the ways we work with such dogs. We try to expose them to as much of everyday life as possible. At the same time, a calm voice and a tender touch is what they need. Many little ones need to be held on our laps for quite a while until they realize nothing is going to harm them.

Being able to put these types down on the ground beside us after time spent in our laps is a major hurdle.

I've had many clients bring us a dog that they say they simply cannot walk. They explain that the dog is just fine in the house or in its yard, but once they try to take it out for a walk, the dog refuses to go or tries to drag the owner back to the house. This is a dog that needs a lot of time and exposure. As with the dominant dog, if you take the time and are laden with patience, you will win and more importantly, the dog will succeed. I have seen so many submissive dogs that complete their training and change their personality … they are very proud of themselves. It is very heartwarming.

BITING

No one wants a dog to bite them. There are a few types of biting, but all should be corrected.

Most puppies play bite. This is learned behavior from when they were with their mother and litter mates. Once the pup comes into its new home and bonds with the family members, play biting will most likely start. It is very easy to correct. Some breeds tend to play bite more than others, such as the Australian Shepherd and Border Collie. These two breeds love to nip at your heels and "herd" you.

We tell all of our clients with puppies not to play rough games such as tug of war with their dogs. This type of game will encourage a dog to bite. As with play biting, the dog is not trying to harm you but if encouraged, it can escalate to the type of biting that does hurt and often breaks skin. So, it is better to discourage the biting from day one than to help develop it.

When a puppy tries to bite you, use your firm voice and tell it "no". You do not have to use sentences. A firm "no" is sufficient and can be used anytime you want to correct your dog. "No" is a basic command that you want your dog to learn. For example, your pup grabs your pant leg and begins to tear at it and growl. You issue a firm command, "Buffy, NO!" This will get the dogs attention. Be prepared to follow it up by giving the dog what she is allowed to chew (bite) and using a pleasant voice such as, "Good girl!"

If the dog drops the toy and goes back for the pant leg, repeat the procedure. If you have a stubborn pup, try elevating the dog. Usually when you pick a dog up he will stop biting. I realize that some dogs are too large to be elevated. In this case, if you try with your voice and it fails to work, you must get a leash and corrective collar. Place the collar on the dog and attach it to the leash. When the dog dives at your pant leg and begins to growl, use the verbal command followed with a quick corrective jerk on the collar. This usually works and may take a few times but consistency will get positive results. PUPSI has had many clients who have a great concern about puppy biting. When puppies arrive to be trained it is almost always a problem area that owners want solved.

Fear biting is another biting problem. Most dog bites come from fear biters. These dogs are easily frightened and easy to spot. They normally drop their heads and tuck their tails. Their eyes look like they don't trust anything or anyone. Many of these dogs have a void past, have come from a rescue situation, or have been in an abusive situation. Since they can't talk to us and give us any background, it is hard to know what has made them this way. Some are timid and fearful from genetics. Working with a fear biter takes a lot of time and patience. Often these dogs only trust their immediate family and never get over their fear around strangers. If the dog has this tendency, and is young, you stand a much better chance of trying to overcome this problem than with an older dog.

Bear is a medium sized little gray dog that came to PUPSI to try daycare and had all the signs of a fear biter. With time and frequent visits to the daycare program, Bear overcame his fears. A few times he tried to sneak in a little "nip" when he was unsure of employees around him, but when all he got back were coaxing words and actions Bear learned he could trust the staff at PUPSI as well as his family. He will always be a cautious dog but he is a lot more trusting and not nearly as nervous due to the work of his owner and his PUPSI caretakers. He has progressed beautifully and lives with and loves five children!!

Obedience training with young fear biters helps a great deal. Not only do they begin to learn commands and enjoy working with their owner or trainer, but the daily routine, including correcting the bad habit, tends to produce positive results. Subjecting a young fear biter slowly and steadily to different situations can help immensely. Individuals working with such a dog must know what they are doing and how to handle it. If you feel you have a fear biter and are not sure how to work with him, seek professional training advice.

Sometimes fear biters are afraid of other dogs and attempt to bite them. These dogs may not be fearful around humans. Again, if the dog is at a young age, it may be possible to overcome his fear of other dogs. Daycare with other canines, gradually getting the dog more and more involved each day, may get rid of the problem.

Unfortunately, the older the dog, the harder it is to overcome fear biting. It is difficult for an abused dog to establish trust. Combine this with age, and you may have a problem that cannot be corrected. As a dedicated dog trainer, I hate to see these cases come along. I am always "for" keeping the dog with the family. There have been countless cases I have not given up on. Most had happy endings. I have watched my son, Trace work with many of these types. He is so patient and will actually get down on the ground with the dog. Putting yourself on their level is very calming to dogs, especially puppies, as we look like big tall trees to them when we are standing up.

The fear biter or the aggressive biter are both problems that must be dealt with. If you own a dog that has aggressive tendencies you must know how to handle the dog. An honest obedience trainer will evaluate your dog and give you his opinion. If you feel the trainer makes sense you need to consider what type of dog you have. Some people think it is important to have a guard dog. Making a dog mean is not something that is hard to do. My question is, why would one want to do that?

In most cases if you own a dog that has a tendency to bite, a dog you do not trust, or one that is very obviously aggressive, you will need to prioritize that problem and get good advice.

SPOILED GROWLERS

Topsy, a cocker spaniel and Andy, a Jack Russell Terrier were very spoiled. Both had been pampered and coddled since day one with their owners. Do not get me wrong, I love to and do spoil all of my dogs. I also make them get off the bed when I want to relax, lie down when I am having dinner, go outside when I think it is time for them to do so. With three grown Alaskan Malamutes in our house all under one roof some sort of order has to be in place. They must behave when it is time for treats and they have earned my trust enough to know that there will be no bad incidents if all three have a bone or toy.

Topsy and Andy had been known to growl if they were asleep on the sofa and an owner walked by or worse, sat down on the same piece of furniture. Andy had even growled at dinnertime if someone passed his food bowl. He had refused to stop begging at the table and if consistent enough, knew he would get a morsel of human food.

Both of these dogs and countless others that have come through PUPSI's doors, have gotten their way most of the time with their owners. The growling has been ignored and therefore, accepted. In these cases, an obedience trainer is almost always needed, as the owner cannot solve the problem that he created.

Most dogs are intelligent enough to test you. If a dog is resting comfortably on your sofa and you are trying to clean the house for a dinner party, moving him may be an effort. If he emits a growl as you approach and you ignore it, the dog has won that round. You may think he looks so comfortable there and decide not to bother him. If he doesn't get up on his own sooner or later and jump down, your second attempt will almost always be accompanied with growls.

Spoiling your dog is great, but establishing boundaries is important. Remember that you cannot reason with a dog. He doesn't understand that lying on the sofa is fine the majority of the time, but when a houseful of dinner guests are arriving, the couch is off limits. If you allow your dog to get on the furniture, you must also teach him the appropriate command when it is time to get off of the furniture.

Yuki, our youngest Alaskan Malamute, is allowed on our bed each and every night. It is by far her favorite place in the house. However, when we say "Yuki, wanna go night-night?" she hops right up, gets down and goes to her corner of the room to lie down. This is something we started doing from the time she was three months old. It is a consistent, nightly ritual, and she knows what is expected of her.

All of my dogs are most definitely spoiled. They do, however, have accepted routines and actions. They understand tone of voice and are easily corrected if they step out of line. They have not taken over in any circumstance. They are showered daily with an abundance of kisses, hugs and love.

You can spoil your dog and still be the boss.

Do not forget that what you allow your dog to do is always acceptable. If you decide you want your dog on the furniture then you cannot let the dog on the couch one day and tell it to get off the next. It is the same with jumping. If you allow your dog to jump on you, then expect your dog to jump on everyone. Decide from the beginning what your ground rules are and go with them. You cannot reason with a dog.

"I'M CALLING TO ASK IF YOU CAN HELP ME WITH..."

The Cary area has over 100,000 residents and continues to grow. PUPSI receives calls daily from dog owners with all kinds of questions. We try to give them the best possible answer to their questions.

Here are some of those questions:

THE BREED OF DOG I SHOULD GET?

How I wish more people would call us BEFORE they get a dog and discuss their family situation, living accommodations, work schedule, lifestyle. I feel certain we could lessen the number of dogs that get returned to the breeder or worse, end up at the shelter. All puppies are cute and many individuals fall for their looks and never investigate the breed or breeds they are acquiring.

It is in your best interest to research the breed of dog you are thinking of buying. If a pound puppy or a mixed breed is your desire, find out what the dog is mixed with and investigate as much about each breed before you make your decision. You could get the best of both breeds or the worst. Do not be in a hurry to get the dog. Believe me, there are plenty of dogs that need homes.

Research is essential. If you are a couch potato who hates exercise, that beautiful blue eyed Siberian Husky is NOT for you. If you've just taken your kids to "101 Dalmatians" and everyone wants a polka dotted puppy, beware: most Dalmatians are not the overly friendly, even tempered canines that the movies portray. If barking gets on your nerves, you will want to stay away from many of the hounds and most definitely the Shetland Sheepdog. We won't even get into dog hair…it comes with the territory in most breeds. Although breeders are attempting to perfect the "hypo allergenic" dog, I'm not so sure that innovation has been entirely successful. Goldendoodles and Labradoodles come with their own set of training issues. You may not be allergic to them, and may not need to vacuum up hair all the time, but you can have a real handful in training these breeds.

Doing as much homework and asking a lot of questions will help you end up with the type of dog you want. Of course your dog will need some training, but if you do your research, you will know what you are in for.

MY DOG JUST ATTACKED MY NEW PUPPY!

We won't go backwards to "dog breed research" but will continue forward. Now you have to put yourself in a dog's world.

IF you have a dog and want another, one of the best things you can do is introduce them on neutral territory. You may have the mildest mannered, laidback canine in the neighborhood. He may sleep on your bed, relax at the front door, greet the mailman, and bring you your morning newspaper. However, your home is HIS domain. God forbid you would even THINK of bringing another

DOG into the mix. You are bringing a dog into his world. Because dogs are pack animals, the majority of the time many of them living together can get along well. Knowing how to add dogs to your family is the key.

The way you introduce your dog to the new canine you want to add to your family is very important. It is best if you go to a playground or an unoccupied school yard or a park with your dog and have another family member bring the new dog. This provides a neutral place to introduce them to each other. Neither of them will consider the meeting place their domain. The place will be new to both of them. Allow them time to sniff and get to know each other. This will give you an immediate sense of how they will get along. If the hair goes up and the teeth show, it may not be a good match. Try again.

If all goes well and you decide to take the new addition home, put the dogs in the same car and go for it. Show the new dog around the house, just as you would if he were your only dog. If growling begins from either dog over existing toys or bones, correct the dog that is showing the negative behavior. Make sure both dogs have bones to chew on and toys to play with.

When a household has more than one dog and the dogs get along, they usually pass chew bones around. It seems that a dog can chew on a bone for a while and then be attracted to the saliva covered one another dog has been chewing on. This is fine and should indicate that the dogs are doing well together.

Always supervise your dog or dogs when chewing a bone – safety is utmost and you will need to be there if any confrontations arise. It is also important to make sure your dog doesn't try to swallow a bone.

I always supervise my three malamutes when they are chewing on bones. They have been around each other for a long time, and they all realize that my oldest, Cuda is the boss. Even so, I never leave them unsupervised with any bones. A challenge can occur at any time. Some dogs will try to chew a bone very fast anticipating that another dog may try to steal it. Watch your dog if he begins to chew really fast as it can be dangerous as the dog will try to swallow large pieces of the bone,

I always tell people to let sleeping dogs lie and to allow a dog to have its toys undisturbed. If your dog is settled in with a chew bone and you want to vacuum, go around it. There are certain toys and bones that you should allow your dog to have. I can't tell you the number of people who always want to take the toys away from their dogs. This is a major no-no. Leave the dog alone, let him have "his" things. An easy way to establish a place for your dogs bones and toys is to put them in basket in one area of a room. This becomes an area that your dog quickly realizes is "his". This area is off limits to humans. This should be something you do for your dog all the time. Do not let children take your dogs things. They are in his place and they belong to him.

Once you have both dogs settled into their home, give both the same amount of attention. Your older dog may be your favorite, and we all have favorites, but in the beginning, take both dogs for walks, give them both treats, shower them both with praise. As time goes by, their individual needs for attention will be understood and both should feel comfortable with their own attention.

Do not allow any negative behavior from either dog. If things go well 98% of the time and you have a problem 2% of the time, do not let bad habits begin. Correct each negative action the dog displays each and every time it happens. If you let the growling dog get away with this type of behavior, you will be creating a long road of correction if you are not on top of the problem from the very beginning. I cannot stress how important consistent correction is for the development of your relationship with your dog. If the dog is allowed to get away with negative behavior towards the other dog, it will build on its success of negative behavior and there will be more problems.

For example, if dinnertime arrives and you place the food bowls down and one dog begins to growl, immediately, using your most serious, lowest voice, correct the dog by saying: "No, Rex!" If this does not work, pick up the food bowls and go get the dog's collar and leash, preferably a nylon choker, depending on the breed of dog. Slip the collar over the dog's neck, place the food bowls down and wait for him to growl again. With this growl, jerk the dog completely off the floor, accompanied with the verbal command. If you are consistent and prepared to do this each time food is placed in front of the dogs, in a very short time, peace will be restored at dinnertime and you will not have to do this again.

Using your collar and leash is one of the best corrective methods you can use. You never place your hands in the middle of a dog fight or offer your hand as a correction to a dog growling at you. The advantage of the leash attached to the corrective collar is that it allows you to successfully correct your dog without any harm to you.

MY HUSBAND HITS OUR DOG!

We stress to dog owners NEVER to kick, hit, or use an object to strike their animals. That shows the dog nothing but negative behavior from you, not to mention hurting your dog. Your hands should only be used to pet your dog, not to harm it. A perfect example of this is the case of the Rottweiler I trained whose owners had continually used their hands to scruff the dogs neck. The message the Rottie got from this was their hands only meant punishment. So, when he grew up he struck back at them. Fortunately, he learned to trust me and we were able to turn this problem around. When they brought the dog to me he was an untrusting canine. He had the idea that human hands coming towards him were going to hit him, scruff his neck, or hold him down. His owners had unknowingly taught him not to trust them. With less than two days in my presence he learned that my hands only gave him warm pats on the head and hugs. By accompanying a pat on his head with a positive tone of voice, he quickly began to trust me. I taught his owners how to use their voices and their hands in a positive way and with time their dog began to trust them. It took time and a lot of patience but it worked.

EVERY TIME MY DOG SEES MY BOYFRIEND OR ANOTHER MAN, SHE PEES!

We often get calls from owners who claim to have the perfect dog except for the submissive urination problem. In breeds such as the cocker spaniel and the dachshund, we always explain that those breeds do have submission problems and tell the owners how to work with it. Many cockers as well as dachsunds never outgrow their problem. The way to begin working with it is to monitor how much water they take in when they are puppies. You should try and greet these little guys outside and use a very calm voice. An excited tone of voice often makes them pee immediately. Often, picking them up causes them to urinate. Try to remember to be very calm and speak in a soft, almost monotone voice when working with them. As they mature, they may grow out of it. Urinating when a dog recognizes someone is another problem entirely.

I had a double problem when a little black cocker spaniel came to me for training. Not only was she a submissive urinator, she was extremely timid when the owner's boyfriend was around. In cases like this, as in all of our training, we ask a lot of questions. If there is a behavioral problem, such as the submissive urination, we try to dig deeper. With this dog in particular it was more than obvious that the dog was scared of the male in the situation. On the first day when both the owner and the boyfriend showed up to go through the pup's training, the dog was immediately timid, with her tail tucked and peeing all over the sidewalk when the man approached her.

We felt there might have been some abuse with this dog, but, as always you need to be extra careful in evaluating the problem. Often people will not admit to any wrongdoing when a dog is concerned. Many times people do not consider hitting a dog, rubbing its nose in waste, or kicking it as "abuse." I mean, after all, it's just a dog, right? WRONG! So, we have to tread very carefully in discussing the dogs problems with the owner. Many times the owner will finally admit to what is actually going on or she may be guessing as to what could have happened.

Reestablishing trust in such circumstances can be difficult. If you are dealing with a person who believes a dog is just some dumb animal, you have a problem. Believe me, there have been many instances where I have wanted to tell the owner to get rid of the human in the relationship and keep the dog, but I have been unable to say this.

With the little black cocker, I reiterated many times in the week of training that hitting, kicking, using a rolled newspaper to "swat" the dog, were all actions that should be stopped immediately. This breed of dog already had a submissive urination problem. The abusive actions were only compounding the problem. Additionally, all yelling at the dog was to be stopped.

Sadly, when the dog was finished with her training, she did well on her obedience but I often felt that the home situation would probably not improve. It was very obvious that the boyfriend was not going to stop abusing the dog. The owner wasn't planning on giving up the boyfriend so I saw no light at the end of that tunnel. The little cocker would probably always have a urination problem.

On a brighter note, we see a lot of puppies that just pee when excited. This is not really submissive urination, but a young pup that hasn't learned to control its bladder. These puppies do outgrow their problem. We advise the owners to learn to control their pups water intake, to greet their dog in a monotone-like voice each time they see their pup and to ask their friends when they visit, no matter how cute the puppy is, to try to maintain a low profile and not "sing" the puppy's name in a high pitched tone. Again, we tell every owner we know how cute their puppy is, and of course we want them to spoil and love their puppy, but when they are dealing with a urination problem, they must "cool it" until the puppy gets a bit older. We also tell them to try and greet their puppy outside as much as possible ... this helps keep carpet cleaning to a minimum.

MY PET STORE PUPPY HAS PAPERS ... I PAID A LOT OF MONEY FOR HIM!

Puppies in pet stores have come from the notorious states where puppy mills thrive. Many states have puppy mills and the seven that are well known for them are Missouri, Nebraska, Kansas, Iowa, Arkansas, Oklahoma and Pennsylvania. These so called "breeders" sell puppies that are pure bred with AKC papers. This is a major case of what I call the "misinformed public." Most of the puppies that arrive from these mills have already had it pretty hard in their short lives. If you get one that hasn't been exposed to negative things, you are fortunate.

Almost all of them will be a housebreaking nightmare. These pups have been taken away from their mother and litter mates at an extremely young age. They have learned to eat, sleep and play in their waste. Many of them have learned to eat their waste. They arrive by tractor trailer to the pet store where they may get their first bath. The pet store cleans them up, deworms them, gives them a quick trip to a local veterinarian for some booster shots, and puts a high price tag on their cage. The misinformed, prospective new owner enters the shop, eyes the "cute" merchandise and makes the purchase.

We see a great deal of these types of new pets at PUPSI. I have seen the same breeder papers on many puppies. Most of the large puppy mills breed all types of pups. They are irresponsible people that have dozens of AKC breeds in their care. They breed the females until they are too old or too sick. Often these dogs never get out of a cage, never see the sunshine or experience grass under their feet. They are literally used until the so called breeder has used them up! Many of these poor animals become so cage bound they actually lose their minds. Many of them spend days pacing back and forth. Some never experience any social contact with humans or other dogs. The short time the females have with their litter is free of any of the mother/pup positive experiences and all too quickly the puppies are taken away and separated from each other at way too young of age. When the new and unsuspecting owner purchases these puppy mill breeds, they cannot understand how they could have paid such a high price for the puppy and ended up with a dog with so many problems. They have fallen for the story the pet store employees tell them and think that they have purchased a high quality pup because they have a piece of paper in their hand that proves the dog came from some great breeder! They assume you get what you pay for. In these cases, they get a whole lot more. Unless they decide to seek out a reputable dog trainer and follow his advice, many of these new pups end up in the local animal shelter.

One of the biggest housebreaking problems we have ever witnessed at PUPSI began with a phone call from a couple who had a dog that was almost two years old that was going to the bathroom inside their house every day. This dog had been purchased as a young puppy from a pet store and eliminated in their house each and every day. They had lived with it for almost two years before they decided to seek help from a dog trainer.

I am not saying that these people just accepted the problem they had, but if they ever got any advice, they never used it. Housebreaking this dog was a long, hard task and educating the owner's was even harder. They had tried so many different housebreaking options, the dog had no idea what was right or wrong. It took us a long time to convince these owners that just because they paid a great deal of money for this pet store puppy that had grown into an untrained adult dog, did not mean the dog would automatically be trainable because it had AKC papers!

PUPSI devoted many hours in working with and helping this dog learn where to eliminate. We had to be vigilant about keeping the dog on a strict schedule and teaching him to go to the bathroom outside. The owners wanted a housebroken dog. Therefore, the use of any pads or papers was gone. They had tried every method of housebreaking the dog and he was extremely confused. With time and our working with the dog with consistency and lots of praise, he accomplished housebreaking.

As I have stressed in the housebreaking section of this book you need to decide what method you prefer and stick to it. Extremely little dogs can often be paper trained or litter box trained. Housebreaking means to teach a dog to eliminate outside. Large dogs should be housebroken. There is a product available now that works great for any size dog, and is especially good for apartment dwellers or people who do not feel comfortable taking their dog for a walk at night. The product is made of pup grass and actually has a tray under it enabling a dog to go to the bathroom on a balcony or other area with minimal clean up problems. The owner can simply discard the solid waste and hose the entire carpet of grass down once a week.

I cannot stress how important it is to know where the dog came from, possibly see the parents, notice how clean the breeder keeps the pups, and investigate the reputation of the breeder. You need to know as much as you can learn about where the dog came from and how it was treated. Even a local shelter has some ideas about the dog they are selling you that they have put up for adoption. You should ask as many questions as you can think of. Most importantly, if you end up with a problem, seek help from a reputable trainer as soon as possible. Don't confuse the dog more than it already is, by trying different concepts and solutions, doing what your neighbor suggests, etc. Get some help!

I CAN'T GET MY DOG TO GO ON A WALK!

Believe it or not, we hear this malady a lot. People cannot understand why a dog refuses to go on a walk or gets away from the house and simply stops and wants to go back. Again, you must put yourself in the dog's place. Where did the dog come from? Was either parent timid, or did you pick the puppy in the litter that hung at the back of the pack, not wanting to socialize? Is the dog afraid of people on the street, other dogs or traffic noises?

Socialization is such a big deal! No matter if you have acquired a puppy or an older dog, getting the dog out and about is a very important first step. Once you get your new dog acclimated to her new home, take her with you to as many places as possible. If the kids go to the school bus stop, take the dog. Ask other children to be slow in approaching your dog and let them pet her one at a time. If your dog is extremely timid, let the dog watch the kids from a distance, getting closer each day. Ask the kids not to be loud and make a lot of quick movements if your dog seems scared.

When you go to the grocery store, take the dog with you. Make sure it is not too hot outside and make the trip a quick one. Let the dog become accustomed to riding in the car and waiting for you. Park where the dog can see you enter the store. Don't be surprised if she is still watching for you in the same position when you return to the car.

Begin walking your dog on short evening walks or early morning, when it is rather quiet outside and the weather is not too warm. Speak to her in a warm tone of voice, and talk to her as you go along. If you sound calm, your dog won't pick up any reasons to be nervous. If a noise startles your dog, reassure her. Stop and pet the dog and let her see that whatever it was that made the noise will not hurt her. Continuous exposure to the sights and sounds of the great outdoors with nothing but positive results will help her more than anything else you can do.

There is a difference between a dominant dog that wants to run the household, including the daily walks, and a dog that is timid about going on a walk. These are two entirely different characters.

The dominant dog is easy to detect. This is the dog that gets up on your kitchen counters, jumps on your bed and refuses to get down, challenges anyone in the house it can, simply lies down and rolls over when you grab the leash to go for a walk. The timid dog often has a submissive urination problem, may shy away from you when you first approach it, is wary of all strangers and once successful with its daily walks may be overly cautious about any change in its daily routine. If you turn down a new street, the timid dog may become fearful.

Treat the timid dog with a lot of patience and kindness. Treat the dominant dog with a firmer hand and a deeper tone of voice. Do not let the dominant dog win. Do not let the timid dog get its way by your feeling sorry for it and giving in. For example, a timid dog may cower and lie down on a walk or act as if any noise scares it. Be calm and sweet, but be the winner in the situation. Do not make a situation worse by losing your temper with a timid dog. Remember, they cannot tell you what made them timid. It is up to you to be patient and attempt to rebuild confidence in a timid dog. This takes a lot of time. Once more, you are the owner, he is the dog. If you have a continuing problem with a dominant dog who walks halfway on a walk, then lies down refusing to move, consult a good trainer. A timid dog will eventually come out of her shell but it takes a lot of patience and positive reinforcement on the owner's end.

CAN MY PUPPY SLEEP WITH THE KIDS?

Of course, your puppy can sleep with the kids. Isn't that what childhood is all about? Every child needs this experience growing up with a dog.

If you have a puppy doing well on housebreaking and he can make it through the night accident free, sleeping with the kids is fine. Make sure that the pup is ready for bed and has been walked or let outside for one last time. Water should have been cut off earlier in the evening and treats put away until the next day. Most puppies love to sleep with children and should settle right in when it is time for bed. Again, consistency is the rule. Try to keep to a certain schedule each night with the pup going outside and then to bed as close as possible to a certain time as you can manage. If you have sleepy heads for children, an adult must assume the responsibility of going in to get the puppy and take him outside first thing each morning.

If your new addition is not quite housebroken and doesn't make it through the night yet, sleeping with the children will have to wait until he is older.

DO YOU THINK MY DOG HAS BEEN ABUSED? HE SEEMS SO TIMID.

Many dogs that are turned in at humane societies have had a horrible previous existence. The poor critters that we find on the side of the road with the sad, hollow eyes are probably both sad and scared. Unfortunately, none of the canines can talk but it is easy to detect happiness and a peaceful demeanor in dogs that are well cared for versus dogs and puppies that have had a difficult life. In many of these cases, a professional dog trainer can really help.

At PUPSI it is usually very easy for us to determine if a dog has been abused, frightened or otherwise mistreated. In the majority of cases we are successful in helping the dog and their family. Of course, we do evaluate dogs with problems that cannot be cured. When an older dog has suffered years of abuse and ends up with a new, loving owner it takes a good long time to work with the dog's fears. Dogs cannot tell us their story, so we have to try and figure it out.

The difficult part is turning an abused, scared dog into a loved, and loving happy dog. We tell owners that sincerely want to love and help their dog that they must start all over, as if they have a brand new eight week old puppy. They must shower the dog with kindness, soft tones of voice and refrain from any type of physical correction. With time, many of these dogs learn what trust means and enjoy warm, loving relationships with their owners. However, in these cases, it really depends on the owner and their devotion to working with these dogs.

Dogs that are extremely timid need a lot of time and patience. You will find yourself being extremely careful in the home, not to drop things or make sudden movements. I have seen dogs drop to the ground that have suffered abuse from a human when given the simple hand command to "stay". Once again, owner participation and a willingness to listen and learn are so important with dogs this timid. These individuals must be completely committed to spending the time they will need to help this animal. Reestablishing trust and teaching the dog what kindness is may take a long time.

In the end the rewards are many. It is wonderful to see the clear, bright eyes of a dog that has learned to trust a human and is able to lie down and sleep peacefully whenever it desires. Those who have helped a dog complete this cycle are true guardians to them. It is very possible to teach a dog love. What you will get in return is an endless supply of warmth, loyalty and companionship. Dogs love you no matter what you wear, no matter who your friends are, no matter what you do for a living. They don't ask questions. Dogs who feel loved and well cared for are always happy to see you.

A 9 year old Golden I taught to walk with a baby carriage

Jimmy, a precious student

Indoor daycare ... before I expanded

Outdoor daycare

Training a little giant!

PROPER NUTRITION

I cannot stress how important proper nutrition is for your dog or puppy. There are so many products on the market that are not good for your dog. You can easily educate yourself on the nutritional needs of your dog. A dog is a carnivore. A dog needs protein. A puppy needs both protein and fat. The majority of the food available in pet stores, grocery stores and even online is full of corn, wheat, rice, fillers, sugar, peanut hulls, beet pulp, feathers, bills, toenails, you name it!

The last time I checked the dog is a direct descendant of the wolf. When wolves kill their prey they shake the intestines in order to avoid eating waste as well as fruits and vegetables that may be in the intestines. You've never seen a dog or a wolf in a corn field eating corn!

It's very easy to do your own research. You will find that many of the brands that are sold in grocery stores, pet stores, online will list the first ingredient as corn. So many of the big companies that produce dog food have plenty of funds available to place eye catching ads on TV as well as in magazines, on radio, etc. that draw you to their brand of dog food. One of the biggest offenders offers a dog food that has two kinds of sugar in it … cancer cells love sugar. Dogs do not need sugar of any kind.

It is also important to switch your dog's source of protein. If we ate chicken all the time we would probably become allergic to it. When you offer your dog different sources of protein you will be avoiding allergy problems. Of course, there are always dogs who seem to develop allergies no matter what. If your dog has an allergy problem I would definitely try different sources of protein before I placed him on a food that wasn't that appealing on the label. Additionally, there are dogs who eat poor quality food their entire lives and live to a ripe old age. My thought is to start your dog on quality food if your budget enables you to and add quality fish oil for his heart and you should be on the right track.

Investigate what is on the label. There are many resources available for helping you feed the right food. A homemade raw diet is tops but often expensive, using as much organic as possible.

HARD DAYS, NIGHTS, MONTHS, YEARS

I've often remarked to friends, clients, veterinarians that I "need more dogs". I cannot remember a time when I didn't "love a dog" although there have been brief periods of time in my life that I have been without the companionship of the wonderful beings I consider them to be. I have literally loved dogs since I can remember. It seems most dogs love me too … there have been very few times when I've met a dog that didn't like me. Even when I am in a situation where I don't know a certain dog, it seems they always find their way over to me, sniff me, wag whatever kind of tail they have, and usually get a pat from me in return. I'm sure I will always have dogs.

Losing them is an entirely different subject. My home is filled with picture albums and framed shots of many of the dogs in my life, present and past. All have been with me at different stages of my life and all hold wonderful memories.

I've shared in the grieving process of many clients and friends who have lost their dogs. None of these stories is easy to tell but each dog lost was completely loved, right up to the end.

TUX

Over the years so many dogs have held a special place in my heart. Many of them have been visitors at PUPSI, not all have belonged to me.

Tux began visiting PUPSI in 1998. He was a beautiful, big Alaskan Malamute that captured all of our hearts. Everyone loved him. When I say everyone, I mean humans and canines. My two Siberian Husky females, Winter and Storm worshiped him. My big male Siberian Husky, Kipper jockeyed for "top dog" placement with him, but considered him a member of the pack at PUPSI.

Tux came to us for dog daycare and boarding. When his owner first walked into the shop I told him, "we don't have any Alaskan Malamutes in dog daycare," because I knew from personal knowledge raising Cuda and Jazz, that once Malamutes matured, they no longer played with other dogs. Tom, Tux's owner, told me his dog liked other dogs, he insisted on it, so we tried Tux out on the playground. Sure enough, he walked around and seemed to fit in just fine.

From that day on, Tux came to PUPSI Monday through Friday and boarded with us whenever Tom and Joyce left town. He was like one of ours. I feel very strongly that dogs recognize their own breeds, or in this case, breeds close to it. Tux and my huskies formed a bond that no one could penetrate. When Tux arrived the first thing in the morning, you could count on hearing his majestic howl followed by the girls' voices on the playground when they saw him walk outside. They would run up to him each day and welcome him. They were always glad to see him.

Tom and Joyce became good friends as well as clients. They lived nearby and I even rescued Tux one sunny day when he got out of their yard and wondered around another neighborhood. He was a bit wolf-like when it came to strangers. Tux would not let just anyone approach him. He enjoyed escaping from his backyard every once in a while in order to wonder through the park near his home. On this particular day, a man contacted the shop and asked if any of us were familiar with Tux because he had him corralled in his yard. I went straight to his rescue and found him locked in a garage, not looking very fond of his situation. The moment Tux saw me, he came right up and got in my car. I returned him to his backyard and checked his escape route: the unlatched gate.

One evening Joyce called our home and asked if we could come take a look at Tux. We went right over and found him with a bit of labored breathing and a very hard stomach. My husband told Tom to take him to the emergency vet immediately. Tom did not know where it was located so we had him follow us. Tux was suffering from gastric torsion or "bloat" as it is commonly called. Fortunately, he made it through the night and came home the next morning.

Tom and Joyce watched Tux closely after that incident and made sure he didn't get any rawhides or bones, tried to observe how quickly he was eating and drinking. When a dog suffers from bloat their stomach actually flips. This is a medical emergency and a vet must be closeby. If a dog has suffered bloat often vets tell owners to be very careful when feeding the dog and make sure the dog eats slowly in small amounts. Vets can actually staple the stomach of dogs in position to avoid bloat Many show dogs have stapled tummies. Dogs that have suffered bloat do not need any extras in their digestive system such as bones and rawhides. Tom and Joyce were very vigilant and fed Tux in small amounts, even giving him an occasional gas pill to make sure his stomach kept in order. They loved their big dog and tried very hard to notice anything out of the ordinary with him. We watched him very carefully at PUPSI.

On February 26, 2006, my birthday, Tux passed away. He had another bout with bloat but this time it was more serious. Everyone was so upset at PUPSI and I cried for weeks. He was a daily part of PUPSI and it was something that took us all a very long time to get over. Tux will always be remembered for his friendly howl and his complete presence. My girls, Winter and Storm looked for him for months. Each time the door to the playground opened in the mornings they watched to see if Tux would appear.

Tux had one particular kennel at PUPSI. It was a very large walk-in that could accommodate his blankets which he needed because as he got older he began to suffer with arthritis. To this day we still refer to it as Tux's kennel and it doesn't take too much imagination to walk by it and still see him there. His friendly howl will always be an echo in the building.

HOLLY – THE ONLY CHOW WE EVER HAD IN DAYCARE

Holly began coming to PUPSI when we did our 3rd expansion in 1995. She was a medium-sized red Chow with a wonderful attitude. At first I was apprehensive about keeping her because the majority of Chows do not get along with other canines and most are one person or one family dogs. Holly proved me wrong on all counts. She was very sweet and got along just fine with everyone.

Holly came to daycare and boarded with us whenever needed. She was a regular on the daycare scene. She only had one problem. Holly suffered from severe separation anxiety. We could only house her in one particular kennel. Anything else, and Ms. Holly Houdini would manage to escape from the kennel and would roam the boarding area keeping her canine friends awake and barking to join her. One particular day on our return from lunch, my husband came to me with an anxious look on his face and indicated I needed to come look at Holly immediately, that she was loose and covered in blood. The blood turned out to be blue kennel paint. One of the employees had put her in the wrong kennel when we went to lunch and sure enough, she had managed, with a great deal of chewing and saliva to get out of it. She must have squeezed herself as tight as she could through the bars because she was covered in spit which had worn the paint off of the kennel. A good bath brought her back to normal.

Holly was such a regular at PUPSI we named a room after her. This also helped employees know exactly where she stayed at breaktime and slept when she was with us overnight. Her separation problem was so severe that her owners had to go to the grocery store and take her with them or risk that their home would be destroyed while they were gone. Whenever they wanted to go to dinner or a movie she usually spent the night at PUPSI. Of course she was with us when vacation time rolled around. Fortunately, she would not make herself sick when she experienced her anxiety at being alone – she simply would not take confinement. She was completely at ease in the kennel she used at PUPSI, but only in that one kennel.

Holly got nasal cancer. I had just read about a study and a treatment Cornell University had done on that particular cancer in canines but her owner's budget did not stretch that far. We still saw her once in a while after her diagnosis then received a call one morning that she had passed away. It was another long heartbreak that all of us had to get over. She was such a good natured, sweet dog.

STORMY AND CORNELIA

For years an elderly lady named Cornelia brought her standard black Poodle, Stormy to PUPSI to board. She was so very fond of him and very particular about his food, one of the best organics available, where he would sleep, and to make sure and bathe him before he returned home. Each time she dropped him off with us, the drill was the same, and she always reminded us of his special "needs."

Stormy was a great dog, never a problem at the kennel, and got along just fine with the other canines. He adjusted very well to PUPSI no matter how lengthy his stay. As the years passed and both he and Cornelia got older, he would stay with us for longer periods of time, as Cornelia began having health issues that would require hospitalization followed by a recovery period. During her illness we would notice Stormy becoming a little depressed and would make sure we made him a special meal or took him on a walk to break up the monotony and keep up his spirits.

Cornelia got very ill and was hospitalized for quite some time. Her daughter dropped Stormy with us indicating at the time that things did not look too good. Weeks passed and Cornelia hung on. We assured the daughter that Stormy was fine and her biggest problem was what to do with the dog once her mother passed. We decided to keep old arthritic Stormy when that time came and try to find someone who would welcome him into their home to pass his final days.

Cornelia did pass away but only after her daughter reassured her that Stormy was at PUPSI and we had plans to take good care of him. Her daughter told us that her mother seemed to hang on for some time and she finally figured out what her mother wanted to know. Where her dear dog was and who would look after him. Once she told her mother about Stormy, she relaxed and passed away peacefully.

A very nice couple with three children and a poodle of their own decided to offer Stormy a home for his remaining days. Although they all tried very hard to make him happy, it seems that he too wanted to leave this world and be with his owner. Stormy passed away not too long after Cornelia. The two were very close and had a deep bond.

IN A MATTER OF WEEKS IN THE FALL OF THE YEAR

PUPSI received word on all three of these wonderful Golden Retrievers below in a matter of weeks. Sweet Nicolas had visited for his last time, stately old Albert a wonderful soul, lost his struggle with arthritis and long time friend Boomer could barely get around during his last visit to the kennel. Each had his own personality and each were blessed with such a sweet presence. All will be greatly missed.

NICOLAS

I shall call this section simply Nicolas as I can't think of enough kind words to describe him. He was a sweet Golden Retriever mix that recently passed away with nasal cancer. Nick was a presence at PUPSI for almost 15 years. We could always count on seeing him during the summer and holiday season. He would jaunt happily into the building with the sweetest look on his face. He was an immaculate boarder and never caused a problem. He had the type of face that prompted anyone to pet and hug him. He will be remembered and missed.

ALBERT

Cut from the same mold as Nicolas, Albert was a perfect gentleman of a Golden Retriever with a huge heart. Never one to cause a moment's problem, Albert lived a good life and was tormented by arthritis. The last time he came to visit he could hardly walk. Still, he never complained and would be labeled as a trooper. We received a sweet note from his distressed owner recently saying he was gone. He was a devoted part of their lives and another old soul that will never be forgotten. While on this earth he had a wonderful life.

BOOMER

Another Golden Retriever that we lost in the same year. Boomer succumbed to arthritis problems just a few weeks before Thanksgiving.

He had appeared on the evening news with us one winter when PUPSI was asked to comment on well trained dogs. Boomer had come to us as a puppy for training and was nothing short of ideal. He learned very quickly and always displayed perfect obedience and perfect manners. He boarded with us whenever his family left town and came to participate in daycare in his younger days.

Losing such members of a family is so difficult. I am just proud to have been a part of each of their lives. They have each left many fond memories.

ROCKET

When my sweet Alaskan Malamute, Cuda was a younger man, a girl stopped by PUPSI and asked if we would consider breeding him with her female. We agreed and charged a stud fee but had said we were not going to take any of the pups. Naturally when the seven pups were born we went to see them. We gave in and took one home and named him Rocket.

Rocket lived at PUPSI and was a typical malamute puppy, playing each day and getting along with the other dogs. Once mature, he lost his desire to play with other dogs and only got along with his small pack. We felt he would be happier in a home with a yard and a good owner so he went to live with one of my husband's friends and his wife. They had a nice home with a huge yard and for a few years Rocket was very well taken care of.

One day my husband stopped by to see his friend and noticed how badly Rocket looked. The man and his wife had split up and with other interests poor Rocket got left out in the shuffle. He no longer had access to the yard and was left in a concrete enclosure with no stimulation, minimal human contact and was being fed horrible food. We were infuriated with the way Rocket looked and immediately took the dog to PUPSI. When I saw him, I cried. He was only ten and looked as if he would pass away at any time.

My son got him in the tub and found a softball size mass under his neck. Of course we contacted Dr. Johnson Russell and he immediately came to see him. Rocket was diagnosed with thyroid cancer and the outlook was grim. Not one to give up on my Rocket I sent all of the results to my holistic vet, Dr. Charles Loops and he began sending him remedies.

Rocket lived with us at PUPSI for another year and 17 days! He was so very loved by all of the staff at PUPSI and he had a home once again. The remedies transformed him into a much healthier looking canine and excellent nutrition certainly played a part.

Rocket is a dog that God gave back to us to make his last days on this earth good ones. So many dogs never get that chance. How anyone can abuse or ignore a dog is beyond me but I am thankful to have compassion in my heart for animals and be so fortunate to put a smile on Rocket's face. When he came back to us he was a very unhappy dog. Once at PUPSI he was simply loved.

OUR D-BOL

Everyone still speaks of this little English Bulldog that passed away in the summer of 2007, doing what he loved the most. Known for his destructive habits, D loved the water and loved to grab and destroy a garden hose. In his 10 years on this earth I cannot count the number of garden hoses he destroyed.

D-Bol was named for a body building steroid and lived up to the label. He was a perfect 65 pounds, with a broad chest and short, muscular legs. He could cross the parking lot quicker than any of the other dogs. He would spy an attendant using a pooper scooper and charge across the play area, jump into mid air and grab the scooper. If it was full or empty was not his concern. Once D got his mouth around the scooper, one might as well give in as it always took at least two people to pry him off. D had the same love for a garden hose. He would jump in the kiddie pools and dive under the water, grabbing the hose. Within minutes water would be squirting from all of the holes his canines put in the hose.

D-Bol had a good life for the breed. His ten years were healthy ones and he lived longer than most English Bulldogs typically survive. He passed away one summer afternoon on the playground after jumping in a pool and playing with the water one of the attendants sprinkled on him from the hose. It seems he had a heart attack because he simply laid down on the asphalt, put his little paw up on our groomer's leg when she went to see what was wrong with him, took a deep sigh, and left this world for a better place. My son tried to give him CPR but it was not to be.

He was always in a good mood with a sunny disposition. Little things pleased him the most.

MY HEART

I have mentioned my Alaskan Malamute, Cuda many times in this book. On April 18, 2011 my dear dog left this earth for his heavenly home. In the last year I experienced many changes and many losses. I knew my sweet friend could not stay with me forever and I tried to prepare myself for the day that I realized would come.

Cuda had done so well the last year of his life. Even though his rear legs were arthritic, with the help of many holistic remedies from Dr. Charles Loops in Pittsboro, NC he made it around just fine. When my husband moved out I noticed Cuda would have a bit of a problem in the yard when he needed to relieve himself. So, I simply got an inexpensive sling made for assisting dogs when they need it. For one year I accompanied Cuda everywhere he went in the yard. With my assistance he felt completely comfortable to resume his old routines. We still went on walks with my staying right by his side, assisting him with his sling instead of his leash.

His last trip to one of his favorite places, the RV park in Myrtle Beach, South Carolina was in July of 2010. He loved to lie in the grass and watch the people and dogs walk by. He always knew whatever was cooking on the grill would be a part of his dinner. When we came home from that trip I had a gut feeling that it may have been the last time he was there.

My boy did a lot more sleeping in the last few months. The screened in porch was what my son fondly referred to as Cuda's Winter Home as the air conditioned dining room became his summer home. The first few months of 2011 were kind to Cuda, staying nice and cool to allow him to stay on his porch. His appetite remained in place and he relaxed on his big dog bed in the cool mornings and cooler nights.

A few days before he left me he seemed to have suffered some type of stroke. With the two rear legs in poor shape he had a difficult time just managing on one, as his front left leg wasn't working at all. His head was tilted to the side and he would look at me as if to ask, what in the world happened? He still had all of his faculties and would not dare to relieve himself on the porch or anywhere other than the yard. We struggled around for three days on my two legs and his one.

My wonderful veterinarian and friend came to the house after his daily work on that Monday evening and Cuda left us in complete peace. I willed myself not to shed a tear as that old soul was so very close to me he would be alarmed that something was wrong. I didn't want him to have any negative feelings or concerns. I simply laid down with him on his massive bed and spoke in his ear about what a wonderful companion and friend he had been to me, how loyal and protective, and that I could never replace him or forget anything he had done for me. I told him a million times or more how very much I loved him. When the time approached for Dr. Russell to get even closer to his procedure, as he had already administered a tranquilizer to relax my boy, I simply covered his eyes with my hand and kept talking to him. When I removed my hand, my dog had the most peaceful look on his face, with both eyes closed.

It was a wonderful, peaceful moment. I know God was so very close to all of us at that time as were many guardian angels.

I thank the dear Lord for giving me such a tremendous friend for 15 years and 10 days. He was a better friend to me than many. I have been so richly blessed to have had a buddy like that in my life for so long.

DOG'S PLEA

Treat me kindly, my beloved friend, for no heart in all the world is more grateful for kindness than the loving heart of mine.

Do not break my spirit with a stick, for though I should lick your hand between blows, your patience and understanding will more quickly teach me the things you would have me learn.

Speak to me often, for your voice is the world's sweetest music, as you must know by the fierce wagging of my tail when your footstep falls upon my waiting ear.

Please take me inside when it is cold and wet, for I am a domesticated animal, no longer accustomed to bitter elements.

I ask no greater glory than the privilege of sitting at your feet beside the hearth. Keep my pan filled with fresh water for I cannot tell you when I suffer thirst. Feed me clean food that I may stay well, to romp and play and do your bidding, to walk by your side, and stand ready, willing and able to protect you with my life, should your life be in danger.

And my friend, when I am very old, and I no longer enjoy good health, hearing and sight, do not make heroic efforts to keep me going. I am not having any fun. Please see that my trusting life is taken gently. I shall leave this earth knowing with the last breath I drew that my fate was always safest in your hands.

If you're alone, I'll be your shadow. If you want to cry, I'll be your shoulder. If you want a hug, I'll be your pillow. If you need to be happy, I'll be your smile. But anytime you need a friend, I'll just be me.

AUTHOR UNKNOWN

A PET'S TEN COMMANDMENTS

1. My life is likely to last 10-15 years. Any separation from you is likely to be painful.
2. Give me time to understand what you want of me.
3. Place your trust in me. It is crucial or my well being.
4. Don't be angry with me for long and don't lock me up as punishment. You have your work, your friends, your entertainment, but I have only you.
5. Talk to me. Even if I don't understand your words, I do understand your voice when speaking to me.
6. Be aware that however you treat me, I will never forget it.
7. Before your hit me, before your strike me, remember that I could hurt you, and yet, I choose not to bite you.
8. Before you scold me for being lazy or uncooperative, ask yourself if something might be bothering me. Perhaps I'm not getting the right food, I have been in the sun too long, or my heart might be getting old or weak.
9. Please take care of me when I grow old. You too, will grow old.

10. On the ultimate difficult journey, go with me please. Never say you can't bear to watch. Don't make me face this alone. Everything is easier for me if you are there, because I love you so.

TAKE A MOMENT TODAY TO THANK GOD FOR YOUR PETS. ENJOY AND TAKE GOOD CARE OF THEM. LIFE WOULD BE A MUCH DULLER, LESS JOYFUL EXPERIENCE WITHOUT GOD'S CRITTERS.

HELPFUL HINTS ON YOUR FOUR LEGGED FRIEND:

- Warm food tastes better. If your dog seems finicky and not really interested in her food, try warming the dry food with hot water or adding hot water to canned food. The warmth releases more odors and the dog usually goes for it. Bone marrow broth is excellent.
- Dogs use their tails to communicate. He usually wags his tail when he sees you or another family member or friend. Dogs usually do not wag their tails when they are alone.
- A sable coat consists of black tipped hairs on top of a different colored background. A brindle coat is similar to a sable coat, but the black tipped hairs form a pattern of irregular stripes. Shetland Sheepdogs and Collies have sable coats and English Bulldogs, Boxers and French Bulldogs have brindle coats. Merle consists of dark patches against lighter backgrounds. If the coat is more of a steely gray color, it is referred to as Blue Merle. Some Australian Cattle Dogs, Collies and Shetland Sheepdogs have these types of coats.

- Tracking dogs put their noses to the ground and need a certain scent, such as an article of clothing, to follow the trail. Air-scenting dogs hold their heads up to sniff the air.
- Wash your dogs bedding in cold water and use baking soda to help eliminate any odors.
- Dogs do experience gas. Try adding enzymes to his food and check the soy content in his food. The better the food, the less gas. (All of my dogs eat organic and are extremely healthy.)
- Be sure to keep all chemicals, make up, antifreeze, alcohol, nail polish and nail polish remover, soap, acne products, make up sponges, pantyhose, dryer sheets, household cleansers out of a dogs reach. Additionally, chocolate and onions are toxic to dogs. Do not give your dog artificially sweetened chewing gum or toothpaste. It can kill them. Certain plants, such as poinsettias are also poisonous. You must always be aware of what is within your dogs reach.
- Noseprints and fingerprints! The outline of a dog's nostrils and the patterns of ridges the nose make are referred to as a noseprint. Many kennel clubs and registries use this identification to help find lost or stolen dogs.
- If your puppy's coat is one color and changes to another when he becomes an adult it is referred to as a strong break. A wiry coat is called broken and the Bulldog and Pekingese have what is called a broken up face.
- The underside of a dog's feet are called pads. Thin pads are called paper feet. Tougher pads are called horny and those able to conquer different surfaces are called heavy or elastic.

- "Muzzle" includes a dog's nostrils, jaw, nasal bones and the section of head in front of the eyes.
- Ever thought about what will become of your dog if something happens to you? The Humane Society offers information on pet trusts and pet estates.
- An evenly placed white band of fur on a dog's shoulders is called a royal collar, the shoulder region a cape and the top of a dog's head a crown.
- Kissing spot, widow's peak, and lozenge all refer to a marking between the dog's ears.
- Over 50% of pet owners in the United States know the name of the neighbor's dog but not the name of the neighbor.
- Dogs can get sunburned as well as frostbite. Dog's with thin skin and pink ears and noses should have sun block applied in the summertime and reapplied if he gets wet. The ears, toes and tail are easily frostbitten. If you think your dog has been exposed to this type of cold, warm up some towels, get the dog to a warm spot and wrap the affected areas. Do not rub the spots. Contact your veterinarian if you suspect either sunburn or frostbite.
- Border collies and herding dogs such as the Belgian Malinois are capable of moves referred to as quicksilver. These breeds have the ability to make abrupt turns, quick starts and sudden stops while maintaining their balance.
- When you see a handler at a dog show moving his dog's legs in a certain position, as well as his tail, it is referred to as stacking. These show dogs have been worked with so much, that this is entirely normal to them. Stacking a dog enables the judge to get a good look at the entire dog.

- When you get ready to give your pooch a bath, make sure you have everything you need. The most important step is to rinse all of the soap and conditioner off of the dog's coat. Be sure to get under the legs and underbelly and tail. Soap can make your clean dog start to scratch!
- The name Chow Chow has no connection to the breed's original Chinese name. The expression came from imported items on a ship. The ship's cargo master would write chow chow instead of listing each cargo item. Soon, dogs on the ships as cargo became known as chow chows. The breed was developed in China more than 2,000 years ago.
- The most popular names for sled dogs are Cody, Niki, Angel, Kira, Max, Storm, Dancer, Juneau, Sacha and Silver.
- Ear mites are eight-legged pests that can get in a dog's ears and multiply into the thousands. Fortunately, they can be cleared up with medication and ear cleaning solutions.
- White German Shepherds are AKC registered but not permitted to be show dogs.
- Wolves are important animals in many Native American cultures. They are respected as teachers and guides to the ways of the wild.
- Jack Russell Terriers are fearless, fun loving and full of energy. They were first bred in England but Americans have lovingly adopted the outgoing breed.
- Modern sled dogs are the best distance runners in the world. Once the distance exceeds ten miles the dog is at the top of that race, meaning it has established its pace and settled into a continuous run. They are endurance dogs. Racing sled dogs can run 4.8 minute miles over long distances.

- The Leonberger is a dog created during the 1800's in the German town of Leonberg. The dog resembles the lion on the coat of arms of the town.
- The Italian Greyhound may be the oldest of the small, lap dogs. They are extremely popular all over the world. Italian Greyhounds look just like the larger Greyhound but are very small and light weight. They have tiny little legs and appear very fragile.
- There are three sizes of Poodle; standard, miniature and toy.
- Dogs use more than a dozen muscles to control their ear movements and locate sounds.
- Despite their size, many Great Danes can be timid and shy around strangers.
- Border collies have herding instincts so strong that they often "herd" family members or children running in a yard.
- A cold, wet nose is a sign that your dog is in good health.
- The "dog days" of summer are named for the alignment of Sirius, the dog star, with the sun as they are seen from Earth.
- Early mornings and late afternoons are the best times to exercise dogs on the beach.
- Some dogs take their favorite toy everywhere they go.
- Dogs can see two colors – blue-violet and yellow. They see many shades of gray.
- The Pekingese from ancient China were sacred protectors of Buddha.
- Images believed to be Great Danes were found on the walls of ancient Egyptian tombs.
- Most terriers are fearless when it comes to other dogs, even ones twice their size.

- When dogs exercise, their tongues become longer due to increased blood flow.
- "Lassie" the beloved Collie, first appeared in a short story in the Saturday Evening Post in 1958.
- Lord Tweedmouth of Scotland bred the first Golden Retrievers as gifts for friends and family in the 1880s.

A FEW A QUOTES ABOUT THE KIND OF LOVE A DOG PROVIDES:

Over the years, many stories have been compiled about our canine friends. Here are just a few of the many wonderful quotes about dogs. These are the kinds of rewards you can expect if you begin a relationship with a dog.

Dogs have many friends because they wag their tails instead of their tongues.

My goal in life is to be as good a person as my dog thinks I am.

The more people I know the more I like my dog.

"When my dog wakes from a dream, I know from his look that I have been present in his dreams." JAMES GARDNER

"A dog is like an eternal Peter Pan, a child who never grows old and who therefore is always available to love and be loved." AARON KATCHER

"*Of course what he most intensely dreams of is being taken out on walks.*" HENRY JAMES

"*Every boy should have two things: a dog, and a mother that allows him to have one.*" ANONYMOUS

In Roman times, only the well to do had dogs. They were considered extremely valuable and were used as guard dogs, hunting dogs, in war and of course, pets. It is said that a Roman governor whose dog that ran away sent an entire Roman army to find her.

"*Properly trained, a man can be dog's best friend.*" COREY FORD

"*Happiness is a ball after which we run wherever it rolls, and we push it with our feet when it stops.*" JOHANN WOLFGANG VON GOETHE

"*When he just sits loving and knows that he is being loved, those are the moments that I think are precious to a dog; when, with his adoring soul coming through his eyes, he feels that you are really thinking of him.*" JOHN GALSWORTHY

"*That would be a low-grade sort of Heaven,
And I'd never regret a damned sin
If I rush up to the gates white and pearly,
And they don't let my Malamute in.*" PAT O'COTTER *A Malamute Dog*

"*If you don't own a dog, at least one, there is not necessarily anything wrong with you, but there may be something wrong with your life.*" ROGER CARAS

"He is very imprudent, a dog is. He never makes it his business to inquire whether you are in the right or in the wrong, never bothers as to whether you are going up or down life's ladder, never asks whether you are rich or poor, silly or wise, sinner or saint. You are his pal, That is enough for him." JEROME K. JEROME

"Happiness to a dog is what lies on the other side of a door." CHARLES OGBURN, JR.

"The best way to make friends with a dog is to talk to him. He can't talk back, but he can understand a heap more than you think he can." WALTER A. DYER

"The most called-upon prerequisite of a friend is an accessible ear." MAYA ANGELOU

"Someone told me that your illustrious friend Goethe hated dogs. God forgive him, if he did. For my part, as you know, I love them heartily. They are grateful, they are brave, they are communicative, and they never play at cards." WALTER SAVAGE LANDOR

"The entire sum of existence is the magic of being needed by just one person." VI PUTNAM

"Dogs are our link to Paradise." MILAN KUNDERA

"Now I see the secret of the making of the best persons. It is to grow in the open air, and to eat and sleep with the earth." WALT WHITMAN

"Everything is perfect coming from the hands of the Creator; everything degenerates in the hands of man." JEAN-JACQUES ROUSSEAU

"When I hear of the destruction of a species I feel just as if all the works of some great writer had perished." THEODORE ROOSEVELT

"Dogs require loving attention, but they give back more than they receive." DOROTHY HINSHAW PATENT

"A friend is a second self". ARISTOTLE

"Dogs are not our whole life, but they make our lives whole." ROGER CARAS

"My little dog – a heartbeat at my feet." EDITH WHARTON

"A man's dog stands by him in prosperity and poverty, in health and in sickness." SENATOR GEORGE VEST

"I can train a dog in five minutes. It's training the owner that takes longer." BARBARA WOODHOUSE

"Whoever said you can't buy happiness forgot about puppies." GENE HILL

"A friend is one who knows you, and loves you just the same." ELBERT HUBBARD

"Yesterday I was a dog. Today, I'm a dog. Tomorrow I'll probably still be a dog." SNOOPY

"The eyes have one language everywhere." GEORGE HERBERT

"Folks will know how large your soul is by how you treat a dog." CHARLES F. DORAN

"No animal I know of can consistently be more of a friend and companion than a dog."
STANLEY LEINWOLL

"Until one has loved an animal, a part of one's soul remains unawakened." ANATOLE FRANCE

"Love me, love my dog." ITALIAN PROVERB

"Every dog must have his day." JONATHAN SWIFT

"Old dogs, like old shoes, are comfortable." BONNIE WILCOX

"The bond with a true dog is as lasting as the ties of this earth will ever be." KONRAD LORENZ

"The more one gets to know of men, the more one values dogs." A. TOUSSENEL

"No one can fully understand the meaning of love unless he's owned a dog." GENE HILL

"A dog has one aim in life. To bestow his heart."
J.R. ACKERLEY

"A dog is the only thing on this earth that loves you more than he loves himself." JOSH BILLINGS

"The average dog is a nicer person than the average person." ANDY ROONEY

"No one appreciates the very special genius of your conversation as much as the dog does." CHRISTOPHER MORLEY

"…he is more faithful even than the most boasted among men; he is constant in his affection, friendly without interest, and grateful for the slightest favours; much more mindful of benefits received…" OLIVER GOLDSMITH, *from A History of the Earth and Animated Nature, 1774*

"Their impression of power is remarkable. They give one the feeling of immense reserves of energy, of great reservoirs of knowledge, of tolerance of disposition, obstinacy of purpose, and tenacity of principle. They are responsive, and they have a lot of quiet, good sense." J. WENTWORTH DAY, *from The Dog in Sport, 1938.*

"With eye uprais'd, his master's looks to scan,
The joy, the solace, and the aid of man;
The rich man's guardian, and the poor man's friend,
The only being faithful to the end."
GEORGE CRABB, *from The Borough, 1810*

"When the Man walked up he said, "What is Wild Dog doing here?" And the Woman said, "His name is not Wild Dog any more,

but the First Friend, because he will be our friend for always and always and always. Take him with you when you go hunting."
RUDYARD KIPLING

"For it is by muteness that a dog becomes for one so utterly beyond value; with him one is at peace where words play no torturing tricks. When he just sits loving and knows that he is being loved, those are the moments that I think are precious to a dog, when, with his adoring soul coming through his eyes, he feels that you are really thinking of him."
JOHN GALSWORTHY, *from* Memories, *1924*

ACKNOWLEDGEMENTS

How to thank so many...please take no offense if I somehow forgot you!

Dr. Jim McDonald, DVM, Woodbridge Animal Hospital, Woodbridge, Virginia for the many appointments and hours spent with you and your wonderful ability to listen, heal and comfort. You are an amazing friend and awesome vet!

Dr. Marty Edwards and Dr. Joy Ganchingco, DVMs, VetMobile and VetCave, Cary NC. For your continuing help and immediate response to any of our calls!

Dr. Johnson Russell, DVM for years of help and advice. Dr. Jim Gallagher DVM, Quartet Animal Hospital, Cary NC for all of the excellent surgeries. Dr. Charles Loops DVM, the one and only BEST holistic vet on the planet!

Dr. Arthur Houts for all of your support; Mimi Clayton; Scott and Renee Shelton and "Molly"; Jan Santel, Autumn Winds Agility; Stamey and Cynthia Peeler for bringing all those dogs to us; Tracy and Julie Barker; David Crump, my wonderful attorney who has left us but was always there for me; our manager Debra who has helped hold down the ship; Mark and Susan Workman; Angie and Doug Schuster and "Raleigh"; Dustin and Christy Norman and "Cooper"; Tom and Joyce Warfield and "Tux"; Tom and Joyce Wood and "Dese"; Earl Thorpe and "Issac"; Van Eure; Kathy and "Bailey" Nigro. My amazing daughter in law, Angelica!